The Role of Reason

in

The Cloud of Unknowing

The Role of Reason

in

The Cloud of Unknowing

A Philosophy of Christian Mysticism

by
DCTopp

Wff

Wyffolden Press

Salem, Oregon

Wyffolden Press

Salem, Oregon

Wyffolden Press publishes Christian works for the thinking person, focusing on philosophy, theology, ecclesiology, science, and current events.

Library of Congress Control Number: 2016920662

Topp, DC
The Role of Reason in The Cloud of Unknowing
DCTopp

ISBN-13: 978-0-9981889-0-4 (paperback)
ISBN: 0-9981889-0-5 (paperback)

Dedicated to my earthly love and helpmate,
Whose patience and encouragement
Enabled the completion of this
Work for my heavenly love.

What is the outcome then?
I shall pray with the spirit and
I shall pray with the mind also;
I shall sing with the spirit and
I shall sing with the mind also.
1 Corinthians 14:15

CONTENTS

PREFACE

My initial interest in the role of reason in Christian mysticism arose from my exposure to two basic groups: church-going Christians who could generally be described as blue-collar charismatics, and non-charismatic Christian intellectuals situated in institutions of higher learning. Actually, prior to my attending seminary, I did not even know there was such a thing as Christian mysticism. My first exposure to the term, then, may go some distance toward highlighting the import and contemporary relevance of this book.

During my first semester at seminary I was in the midst of a Contemporary Philosophy course in which a discussion arose concerning the feasibility of language-independent thought. As the discussion went to and fro, I could not help but think of personal experience I had had in that vein, and so I spoke up, informing the small group that, "During efforts to deepen my interaction with God in the past, I regularly experienced great frustrations. As I groped for unencumbered intimacy with Him, I found myself consistently stymied by the limits of vocabulary. Once I reached a certain level of intimacy, I seemed restrained from further advance by the very limits of the language I was using. If I could somehow circumvent language, I thought, then perhaps..." I got no further. Peering at me from under a furrowed brow, the professor cut me short by saying, with a noticeable degree of defensiveness in his voice, "I'm not a mystic!" Okay, I thought. Immediately sensing that I had touched a nerve, I went no further with my disclosure. The professor was not a mystic, and by implication he believed that what I was in the midst of relaying was something 'mystical.' But even more, he also implied that mysticism was something he found threatening, if not improper.

Though the above scenario is perhaps not overly remarkable in and of itself, it becomes so as contrasted with previous experiences I had from the other end of the spectrum. Let me explain.

Prior to re-commencing my education at the seminary level I pastored a cooperative of HomeChurches in Northern California for over five years. My constituents were almost exclusively blue-collar, with minimal if any education beyond that of high school. We were also of a decidedly charismatic stance; that is, we believed and acted upon the belief that the gifts of the Holy Spirit, as mentioned in the Bible, were intact. But the charismaticism we practiced, as is likely the case with most of such a disposition, went further than just a belief in and practice of the spiritual gifts. It included a deep spirituality, or what some may call (I came to discover), mysticism. It included a belief in and involvement with the very near and active presence of God – an unmediated link to the Absolute, if you will. My point here is not to explicate the intricacies of such beliefs and practices, but to indicate the basic socio-spiritual backdrop with which I was involved, for the following reason: Though such people and such an environment have many positive features, there was one attending feature which was not so positive: My congregation (and other congregations of the same ilk with which I had to do) consistently spurned 'things of the mind,' or significant intellectual engagement of any type. Their opposition to such was often so intense it could be described as militant.

Through my exposure to and interaction with people of a blue-collar charismatic disposition, I came to conclude that their rejection of intellectual engagement[1] was generated by several factors: intimidation, mistrust, and a particular view of spirituality. Because of their limited education, and in some cases, limited intellects, anyone who presented spiritual information with a significant degree of intellectual content was perceived as *arrogant* ("You are just trying to show us how smart you are."). And because such intellectual engagement was liable to push the limits of their mental abilities, the data presented by the intellectual could not, they assumed, always be sufficiently assessed. Thus, they found it *intimidating*. It was, or at least they thought it was, beyond their reach. And when 'the arrogance factor' weighed-in with 'the intimidation factor,' one result was mistrust: "How can an arrogant person who speaks over our heads be trusted?" To make matters worse, a general notion which prevailed was, "The intellectual and the spiritual do not mix. Whatever is of the mind is not of

---

[1] I am purposely avoiding use of the term 'intellectualism,' because of its connotation of "over-indulgence in the things of the mind." The anti-intellectual militancy I am referring to does not correspond with over-indulgence with the things of the mind, but with 'things of the mind' in general.

In a similar vein, 'intellection' will not do here, as the group referred to would not object to 'thinking'; they realize that thinking is necessary for normal human functioning. Rather, what they object to is substantive thinking on spiritual issues which extends beyond the familiar or beyond their comfort level. It is extensive, deep, or systematic thinking to which they object.

the spirit. And whatever is of the spirit is not of the mind. And as the spiritual is superior to the mental, the mental must be rejected."

Given, then, my experience of pastoring in such a setting, it was in one respect a great shock, and in another respect a great revelation to come upon the attitude of the seminary philosophy professor (an attitude which I have since, numerously encountered in the seminary environment). It seemed to me that I had discovered two great poles in Christianity. On one end of the pole lie those who embrace 'the mystical' to the exclusion of, with apprehension of, and with animosity toward the intellectual. On the other end lie those who embrace the intellectual to the exclusion of, with apprehension of, and with animosity toward the mystical.

I recognize that the above characterizations are just that – characterizations. Not all Christians abide in either of the specified camps. Certainly, not all blue-collar charismatics are anti-intellectual, just as not all academics are threatened by deep spirituality. Nevertheless, the significant presence of both groups have been noted, or exemplified, by Christian thinkers at large. In his book, *Love God with All Your Mind*, J. P. Moreland points out the rising trend of anti-intellectual sentiment within Christian ranks. He quotes R. C. Sproul:

> We live in what may be the most anti-intellectual period in the history of Western Civilization... We must have passion – indeed hearts on fire for the things of God. But that passion must resist with intensity the anti-intellectual spirit of the world.[2]

---

[2] J. P. Moreland, *Love God with All Your Mind* (Colorado Springs: NavPress, 1997), 19.

On the other end of the spectrum, Arthur L. Johnson, a non-charismatic doctor of philosophy (read: intellectual), in his *Faith Misguided: Exposing the Dangers of Mysticism*,[3] represents mysticism as something to be totally shunned. 'Christian mysticism' is a misnomer, a misrepresentation of reality which places experiences and emotions above the word of God. And charismatic Christianity, Johnson says, is the zenith of this perversion.

In any case, the purpose of this book is not to conduct a comprehensive survey of Christians to discern who and how many lie where on the spirituality versus intellectualism spectrum. Rather, my purpose is to explore the relationship between Christian mysticism and the intellect, or more exactly, between Christian mysticism and the primary operant of the intellect – reason.

Because the paths one could take in investigating the relationship between Christian mysticism and reason are many, and because space and time are limited, this investigation will chiefly be confined to and emanate from one primary source, a noted and anonymously written fourteenth century piece of mystical writing entitled *The Cloud of Unknowing*.

It is my intention, via examining the role of reason in *The Cloud of Unknowing*, to contribute understanding to both the scholarly and ecclesiastical communities regarding a healthy relationship between reason and Christian mysticism. Through examining this particular mystical text, I hope to help

---

[3] Arthur L. Johnson, *Faith Misguided: Exploring the Dangers of Mysticism* (Chicago: Moody Press, 1988).

soften the contest between spirituality and reason in the Christian community by transforming that contest into the concert
the Bible portrays it as. God has given us minds, and expects
us to use them. God has given us spiritual capacities, and expects us to use them.

As *The Cloud*, in most respects, represents a radical but
legitimate form of Christian mysticism, my approach will be
to highlight and defend those elements which are viable, while
acknowledging and attempting to mend its extreme expressions.[4] This will be accom-
plished through comparing
and contrasting the role of
reason in the mysticism of
The Cloud of Unknowing
with that advocated in the
Bible, treated in secondary

> **God encourages Chris-
> tians to embrace both
> the dynamism and
> mysticism of the Spirit,
> and the rule and ration-
> ality of the Word.**

theological and philosophical works, explored in other mystical approaches, and encountered through my personal insights
and experiences. In brief, I believe we will discover that God
encourages Christians to *embrace both the dynamism and mysticism of the Spirit, and the rule and rationality of the Word.*
While encounter with the Spirit of the living, personal God of
the Bible is dynamic (characterized by power, surrender, and
degrees of unpredictability) and often mystical (mysterious,
supernatural, and partially suprarational), such encounters
must begin and end with Bible-based rational activity. The
object, means, and results of Christian mysticism must square

---

[4] "Viable" and "extreme" expressions of Christian mysticism will obviously need defining and defending, but such work comprises much of
the body of this thesis, and will thus, not be detailed here.

with the plain proclamations of Scripture.[5] Thus, it is the 'concert' of mysticism and reason which results in maximal edification of Christian believers and their communities.

DEFINING TERMS

The following should be viewed as common starting points, working definitions which can be refined as needed in the body of this work.

Spiritual, spirituality, and mysticism are all related terms which refer to various aspects of one end of the spectrum in question. In broad strokes, *mysticism* signifies the quest for union or communion with the mysterious Reality which lies beyond the sensible, corporeal realm. Notions of what comprises that Reality vary in keeping with worldviews. As this book is written from a Christian worldview, the working assumption is that the biblical God is the ultimate reality.[6] The question of whether *union* or *communion* with the Ultimate is to be sought also tends to depend on worldviews. This question will be addressed primarily in chapter five.

While mysticism refers to the quest of that Reality which lies beyond the sensible, corporeal realm, it is that Reality and its associated realm which is here to be understood as *spiritual*.

Spirituality, then, is very similar to mysticism, as both refer to an active effort to significantly interact with the supernatural, supracorporeal realm. The primary difference in the

---

[5] The word of God is not only presented in *rational* language, but productive personal embrace of it necessitates aligning oneself with its *rule*. That is, the Bible provides a plumb-line by which the thoughts, words, and deeds of all believers are to correspond.

[6] In chapters four and five, argument will be forwarded as to why this assumption is superior to others.

terms, as commonly under-
stood, is that mysticism is
a radical form of spirituality. All mystics are spir-
itual, but not all spiritual persons are mystics.

> **All mystics are spiritual, but not all spiritual persons are mystics.**

On the other end of the spectrum, *reason*, as used in this writing, will be construed as those communicable capacities, methods and means by which a mind interacts with that which is conceived. By 'communicable,' it is to be understood that respective reasoning processes can rightly be represented to, and consequently duplicated by others, akin to the repeatability dimension of 'the scientific method.' That is, although reasoning cannot occur independent of respective subjects, there remains an objective, communicable feature to it. And while the particular capacities, methods and means of reasoning vary widely, from abstracting, comprehending, relating, and differentiating, to inferring, deducing, and inducting, particular forms of reasoning will only be addressed as needed.

Mind refers to that sphere of each rational being in which reasoning occurs. Taking up the 'mind-body problem' – whether the mind is localized in and is solely a product of the material brain – is beyond the scope of this work. It will be assumed, however, that the mind is a subset of and a capacity of the human spirit.

PROBLEMS AND ISSUES WHICH WILL NOT BE
ADDRESSED

Though sufficient contextual information will be supplied in chapter one regarding *The Cloud's* authorship, intended audience, historical context and so forth, the depths of literary or textual concerns will not be plumbed. It is not my intent to speculate, as do many *Cloud* researchers, on the identity of its anonymous author.

Further, it must be acknowledged that *The Cloud* does not represent Christian mysticism as a whole – no piece of literature does. As a prominent example of Christian mysticism, however, *The Cloud* will duly serve as a catalyst by which the contemporary contest between mysticism and reason can be addressed.

PREVIOUS DISCUSSION ON THE TOPIC

No identified sources deal specifically with the role of reason in *The Cloud of Unknowing*, nor have any used *The Cloud* to address the contemporary contest between mysticism and reason in the Christian community at large. However, treatments of the interaction between reason and mysticism can be unearthed in the Bible, and in works on mysticism, philosophy of religion, reason and reasoning, thought and thinking, rationalism, faith and reason, intuition, and theory of religious knowledge.

AVAILABLE PRIMARY AND SECONDARY SOURCES

Both original editions of *The Cloud of Unknowing* and translations into contemporary English are available. As *The Cloud* was composed in fourteenth century England, the autograph was written in Middle English. Because little meaning is lost in translations to modern English, the modern form will be utilized in this work. The primary translation which will be referenced, William Johnston's *'The Cloud of Unknowing' and 'The Book of Privy Counseling,'* published by Doubleday, in New York, 1973, is based on the critical text of Professor

Phyllis Hodgson, having been edited from the manuscripts with introduction, notes, and glossary, *'The Cloud of Unknowing' and 'The Book of Privy Counseling,'* Oxford University Press, 1944.

CHAPTER ONE

INTRODUCTION TO *THE CLOUD OF UNKNOWING*

HISTORICAL BACKGROUND AND CONTEXT

The Cloud of Unknowing is one of Western civilization's spiritual classics, and its author is counted by some as "the most subtle and incisive, as well as the most original, spiritual writer in the English language."[7] But from whence did this masterpiece come, and who is its lauded author? Though the former can be answered with some exactitude, the latter remains largely shrouded, and that intentionally, in mist.

The oldest extant manuscript of *The Cloud* dates from the early fifteenth century, but gives evidence of being written slightly earlier.[8] As its contents were well known by the young Walter Hilton, and given its literary peculiarities, *The Cloud* must have been authored between 1345-1386, most likely the latter end of this span. Internal and linguistic evidence suggests the manuscript arose from England's north-east Midlands,[9] being penned by an educated man with a substantive theological background; very possibly a university graduate.

---

[7] Barry A. Windeatt, *English Mystics of the Middle Ages* (Cambridge: Cambridge University Press, 1994), 67.

[8] David Knowles, *The English Mystical Tradition* (New York: Harper & Row, 1961), 70-71.

[9] Windeatt, *English Mystics*, 67.

He was likely a recluse. The blessing given at the end of the writing intimates he may have been a priest,[10] though no sign is given of allegiance to a particular religious order.

Several motives may be attributed to the author's choice of anonymity. The most likely of these corresponds with counsel lent by the author in the writing itself; namely, that those things which are not God are to increasingly fade from focus; and that humility, being a prime virtue, can well be expressed by the absence of effort to elevate oneself in the eyes of the world. By refusing to divulge his name, *The Cloud* author practices what he preaches. Exuding the wisdom he does, in a form that has been acknowledged and honored and consulted for centuries – in essence, generating a best-seller – while at once refusing to take credit for it, the Englishman certainly does exhibit a humility and selflessness. One could well wonder how many contemporary Christian authors or recording artists would be willing to do the same.

Windeatt, however, believes that *The Cloud* author's anonymity can best be attributed to the spiritual and literary tradition out of which it arose.[11] Being an heir to the *Mystica Theologia*[12] of Pseudo-Dionysius the Areopogite,[13] Windeatt holds that the author's anonymity is simply an expression of his adherence to Pseudo-Dionysius' *via negativa*.[14] If one can express nothing positive of God, how can positive self-expressions be legitimized? But Windeatt's reasoning seems to fall short, in that while *The Cloud* author certainly adheres to the

---

[10] Ibid.
[11] Ibid.
[12] Latin for "Mystical Theology."
[13] C. 500 AD.
[14] Latin for "negative way."

via negativa, as shall be evidenced later, such a negative road demeans only the efficacy of positive assertions of God, not of His creations.

In any case, that *The Cloud* author managed to remain anonymous is remarkable, especially in light of the attention and criticism the book attracted immediately after publication.[15] As alluded to above, it is evident that *The Cloud* author and Hilton had degrees of interaction and mutual criticism. And while *The Cloud* is commonly reckoned the first of his writings, it is widely held that the Englishman went on to publish *The Book of Privy Counseling*, *The Epistle of Prayer*, *The Epistle of Discretion*, two translations of *Denis Hid Divinity* and *Benjamin Minor*, and a paraphrase of two sermons of St. Bernard entitled *Of Discerning of Spirits*.[16]

In retrospect, it should be no great surprise that a piece such as *The Cloud* should rise from the misty lochs of fourteenth century England and Europe. It was after all, unlike today, a deeply religious land. *The Cloud* author and his public could "take for granted a Church, a faith, and a sacramental life that are no longer accepted without question by many of his readers today."[17] It was a time and a place which produced not only the anonymous Englishman, but Richard Rolle, Walter Hilton, Julian of Norwich, Margery Kempe, Richard Methley, Meister Eckhardt, Henry Suso, Jan van Ruysbroeck, and Catherine of Siena. Thus, regarding Christian mysticism, the fourteenth century has no rival, save perhaps the sixteenth,

---

[15] Knowles, *Mystical Tradition*, 68.
[16] Ibid., 67.
[17] William Johnston, *The Cloud of Unknowing and Book of Privy Counseling* (New York: Image Books, 1973), 29.

with Teresa of Avila and John of the Cross.

Of the English mystics, Rolle and Hilton managed a much wider readership than either *The Cloud* author or Julian. And while there are signs of exchange between them, each author exhibits distinctive approaches and styles, replete with different aims and assumptions.[18]
Even so, there remains something of a unifying theme amongst medieval English mystics – pursuit of intimacy with God through love, along with a desire to share both the methods and the fruit of such pursuit.

> **Neither knowledge nor its effective dispersal must be mistaken for the aim itself – to move the attention of the soul toward God.**

Knowledge or learning for its own sake is dismissed as impotent for such a task.[19] Neither knowledge nor its effective dispersal must be mistaken for the aim itself. *The Cloud* author emphasizes this point, warning against mistaking the pleasures or literary proficiency of the writing itself for the writing's aim – to move the attention of the soul toward God.[20]

While these writers seemed to recognize that the demands of the spiritual disciplines they proffered would preclude all but the committed, they at once hoped that a growing contingent of their contemporaries would find it appealing. Their hopes were not unfounded. The time seemed ripe for a move such as this. Fourteenth century England was as if groomed to both generate and propagate Christian mysticism. There abode a general discontent amongst the populace, spurred by

---

[18] Windeatt, *English Mystics*, 2, 4.
[19] Ibid., 1, 2.
[20] Ibid., 6, 7.

plagues; economic recession; scarcity of labor; diminished agricultural, pastoral, and wool-trade expansion; war; the rising of the peasants in 1381; attacks upon traditional

> **Fourteenth century England was as if groomed to both generate and propagate Christian mysticism.**

Catholic theology by Wyclif; and the rise to consciousness of English nationhood.[21]   On the other hand, notable advances were being made in the arts, architecture (Gothic spires and towers), speculative thought (Duns Scotus, William of Ockham), and literature (Langland and Chaucer). In keeping with Ockham, thought in the universities turned from metaphysics, natural religion, Thomistic attempts to integrate philosophy and theology, reasoned conclusions and revealed truth. Human reason could no longer make pronouncements upon the nature of God. Thus, human minds were influenced to turn toward a mystical approach to faith. This mystical train of thought was pushed along by the reintroduction of Neoplatonic and Dionysian thought. Literature took on an inward looking character. The true mystic need not look to other humans, but is taught and led by God.[22] The subsequent appearance of religious movements appealing to commoners, including that of mystical contemplation, was to set the stage for the Reformation in England.

It was a world distinct from the monasticism of the twelfth century and pietism of the fifteenth century. "The religious climate of the age was sympathetic to a personal and 'mystical' approach to the way of perfection."[23] The ark in the flood

---

[21] Knowles, *Mystical Tradition*, 39.
[22] Ibid., 42.
[23] Ibid., 23.

mentality of monasticism gave way to personal and often solitary endeavors. Whereas in the preceding centuries, per the force of the centralized Roman Church, all literature was composed in Latin, and its works confined to clerks, monks, and canons, the fourteenth century initiated a great change. Latin was increasingly translated into English (Middle English). Writings became more personal and directed toward specific individuals or lower levels of the literate public. For the first time masters could instruct their disciples, and mystics describe their experiences in simple, informal, non-conventionalized, common vernacular.

And whereas doctrine had been formalized by nine centuries of use since Augustine, being traditional and general in form, it lacked the personal touch, urgency and immediacy characterized in the desert Fathers. Many of the devout existing outside the established religious order had for years longed to revisit such a deep spirituality, with limited means by which to do so. In the fourteenth century, Christian mystics, in correspondence with the impetuses and opportunities of that era, went a long way toward satisfying that longing.

> **Whereas doctrine had been formalized by nine centuries of use since Augustine... it lacked the personal touch, urgency and immediacy characterized in the desert Fathers.**

Its Inspiration and Influence

It is of value to note that *The Cloud* author not only refers to Scripture with regularity, but also to giants of the faith, such as Augustine, Dionysius, Gregory, Bernard, Aquinas, and

Richard of St. Victor. Also, there are striking similarities be-tween the Englishman's work and that of St. John of the Cross. Although St. John abode some two centuries later, it can be said of the Englishman, "that almost every detail of his doc-trine is paralleled in the latter Spanish mystic – and not only the doctrine but even the words and phrases are in many cases identical."[24] Thus, *The Cloud* author was not only influenced by prominent Christians of the past, but influenced prominent Christians of the future.

The Englishman belongs to an 'apophatic'[25] theological tradition, as he believes God is best known by negation. This tradition was influenced by Neoplatonism, Gregory of Nyssa and Dionysius the Areopagite. It is the latter to whom the Eng-lishman primarily defers, and understandably so, as medievals considered Dionysius a convert of the apostle Paul who, ac-cordingly, spoke with an authority close to that of Scripture. Only of late has it been established that Dionysius was actually a Syrian monk of the sixth century. Thus, it was *Pseudo*-Dio-nysius and his *Mystica Theologia* from whom the Englishman admittedly derived aspects of his treatise.[26]

According to Pseudo-Dionysius, because God is beyond normal human means of investigation or representation, such as concepts or symbols, He can only be joined through a *via negativa*, in which the senses and intellect are bypassed. The soul is then "united with the 'ray of divine darkness' and

---

[24] Johnston, *The Cloud*, 30.
[25] From the Greek, αποφατικη, "to mark out or distinguish by taking away."
[26] Johnston, *The Cloud*, 139.

comes to know God through unknowing."²⁷ Parallels in phraseology with *The Cloud* author are obvious, even as those of
theme shall be, as explored below.

Intended Audience

Though initially written for a 24 year old disciple,²⁸ *The
Cloud* author anticipated that the work might be circulated.
Given that possibility, and the spiritually intense nature of the
piece, the Englishman set out clear parameters by which potential readers could determine their fitness to engage the text.

Those who yet satiate themselves by means of the flesh
are immediately disqualified. Those who would read the book
must be sober-minded, not merely curious. They must feel the
tug, "the mysterious action of the Spirit in their inmost being
stirring them to love."²⁹   Readers must have proven themselves faithful in the good works of 'the active life,' and have
a desire to go on from there, graduating unto the inner depths
of contemplation.³⁰   Prospective contemplatives should be
without peace in their current works, being driven to fix their
love upon God in a more significant way. And if these tests
are passed, "Anyone disposed toward contemplation will recognize something akin to his own spirit when he reads this
book."³¹

---

²⁷ "Dionysius the Pseudo-Areopogite," in *The Oxford Dictionary of the
   Christian Church*: 3rd ed., Oxford: Oxford University Press, 1997.
²⁸ Johnston, *The Cloud*, 45, 51.
²⁹ Ibid., 44.
³⁰ 'Contemplation' and 'the active life' are both key, technical terms in the
   Englishman's presentation, and will thus be defined in the section,
   "Thesis of *The Cloud*."
³¹ Johnston, *The Cloud*, 143.

CONTENT OF *THE CLOUD*

The 75 short chapters which comprise *The Cloud of Un-knowing* are intended primarily to instruct but also to inspire those who long to take-up 'the contemplative life.' While the author's own mystical experience remains largely un-described, he lends direction for contemplation to his young pupil, as well as others he suspects will read the book. *The Cloud*'s particular "recipe of the spiritual life"[32] centers on the relation between the soul and God. 'God' is assumed to be the Christian God of the Bible.

THESIS OF *THE CLOUD*

The purpose of *The Cloud* is to lead its readers to practice and perfect that most noble, effectual, and significant of spir-itual works – contemplative prayer. It is through contempla-tive prayer that God can most fully be known by humans this side of heaven.

While it would be unfounded today, the Englishman as-sumes his readers know of 'contemplation.' It was apparently well known, at least in Christian circles, that contemplation was a markedly high and markedly deep discipline taken-up by those who were most earnest in their quest for intimacy with God. In keeping with this, and as specified above in the author's list of qualifications for prospective readers, it is the rare individual who is ready to take up contemplation. The faint of heart, the undevout, and the irresolute need not apply.

---

[32] Knowles, *Mystical Tradition*, 69.

Though the Englishman's readers may have heard of contemplation, its potency, and of the lofty spiritual status of its
practitioners, it is clear that they knew nothing of its substance
or workings. It was to them a black box. What is witnessed
in *The Cloud*, then, is its author opening up the black box
called 'contemplative prayer,' explaining its workings, and en-
couraging his pupils to explore its dimensions.

Contemplative Prayer

"The very heart of this work is nothing else but a naked
intent toward God for his own sake."[33] This type of intensely
focused prayer has only one 'intent' – encounter with God.
That intent is to be 'naked' – divested of anything which is not
God. All else is to fall to the wayside: self, other creatures,
concerns, pleasures, pains, thoughts, and most remarkably,
even thoughts of God.

Perhaps the best exemplification of the radical nature of
the work is that even the most
holy of thoughts – those of God
– are to be laid aside. Though
many would surely count this
as excessive and even dangerous, *The Cloud* author gazes
beyond such doubts and criti-

> *The Cloud* author
> gazes to a rarely seen
> truth – that God
> Himself is much
> more precious than
> our thoughts of Him.

cisms, to a rarely seen truth – that God Himself is much more
precious than our thoughts of Him.

Correspondingly, the Englishman reminds his students
that God cannot be possessed by knowledge. If it is God we
are after, and not mere thoughts of Him, such thoughts can

---

[33] Johnston, *The Cloud*, 80.

prove to be distractions. Only love and a naked intent, divested of all material, spiritual, and conceptual baggage, will succeed.[34] All clear conceptualizations must be rejected as they arise "during the blind work of contemplative love."[35] In contrast to clear thoughts, the Englishman says, "this one loving blind desire for God alone is more valuable itself, more pleasing to God and to the saints, more beneficial to your own growth, and more helpful to your friends, both living and dead, than anything else you could do."[36]

However, as this prayer is practiced, it may initially yield nothing but "a kind of darkness about your mind, or as it were, a cloud of unknowing."[37] But the initiate is to persevere until joy is felt in it. In other words, the initiate may:

> feel nothing except a naked intent toward God... Try as you might, this darkness and this cloud will remain between you and your God. You will feel frustrated, for your mind will be unable to grasp, and your heart will not relish the delight of his love. But learn to be at home in this darkness... If in this life, you hope to feel and see God as he is in himself it must be within this darkness and this cloud.[38]

We finally get a glimpse of just what the author means by that mysterious phrase, "the cloud of unknowing." When he speaks of darkness and of a cloud, he is not hoping to spark some image in the mind of the seeker. Rather, 'darkness' and 'cloud' refer to the absence of knowledge; that which cannot

---

[34] Ibid., 136.
[35] Ibid., 60.
[36] Ibid.
[37] Ibid., 48.
[38] Ibid., 48-49.

be seen with the mind's eye; hence, the cloud of *unknowing*.[39]
It is this darkness of unknowing which lies between the contemplative and God.

As thoughts and all other things which are not God are
laid aside, initiates will cer-
tainly come to experience
this state of unknowing, of
darkness and cloud. It will be
unusual, uncomfortable, un-
nerving. But if initiates hope
to encounter God as He is,
they must persevere in the

> As thoughts and all
> other things which are
> not God are laid aside,
> initiates will come to
> experience this state of
> unknowing, of dark-
> ness and cloud.

face of the darkness, for it is only through such dark clouds of
unknowing that God can ever be known.

The cloud of unknowing, however, is not the only cloud
with which the contemplative must deal. Just as that cloud lies
between the contemplative and God, so a 'cloud of forgetting'
must abide between the contemplative and every created
thing.[40] Because all of creation, including thoughts, concepts,
and images, are not God, they must be laid aside in the prayers'
quest for God. All created things must be buried beneath a
cloud of forgetting, while the seekers' naked love rises upward
toward God. It is there, with the cloud of unknowing above,
between the seeker and God, and the cloud of forgetting below, between the seeker and all creatures, that the seeker experiences the *silentium mysticum*,[41] about which the Englishman read in the work of Pseudo-Dionysius.[42]

---

[39] Ibid., 53
[40] Ibid.
[41] Latin for "mystical silence."
[42] Johnston, *The Cloud*, 9.

The contemplative must then be ready for hard work. The primary labor is:

> the unrelenting struggle to vanquish the countless distracting thoughts that plague our minds and to restrain them beneath that 'cloud of forgetting'... This is the suffering. All the struggle is on man's side in the effort he must make to prepare himself for God's action, which is the awakening of love and which he alone can do.[43]

So in this great struggle, contemplatives must rely upon and wait upon God's action. The initiative rests with God. Seekers are dependent upon His grace.[44] Duties or rituals of supposed holiness, or even the sacrifice inherent in mystical pursuits, produce nothing in themselves but facades of intimacy with God. But every now and then, as the seeker waits with cloud below and cloud above – if God is merciful and the seeker patient – God will break through! Many contemplatives turn back too soon. Once they encounter the intimidation of the darkness, they turn back to easily accessible thoughts of worldly pleasures, unaware of the glory which awaits them, of "the spiritual comfort which would have succored them had they waited."[45]

> He who patiently abides in this darkness will be comforted and feel again confidence about his destiny... And finally there will come a moment when he experiences such peace and repose in that darkness that he thinks surely it must be God himself.[46]

---

[43] Ibid., 83.
[44] Ibid., 68.
[45] Ibid., 137.
[46] Ibid., 138.

CLOUD COMPONENTS

Complaints which arose from the Englishman's Christian contemporaries with apparent regularity concerned the purported value of contemplative prayer. Is it not excessively spiritual? Is it not so preoccupied with the heavenly that it is of no earthly good? And as a result, does it not fail to fulfill many of the Lord's commissions regarding earthly ministry? Provocatively, the biggest critics, the Englishman says, tend to be those most zealous and active in the Christian life.[47] Nevertheless, *The Cloud* author speaks straight to these criticisms.

Kinds of Christian Life

The value of the deep spirituality inherent in contemplative prayer can be better appreciated when set within the context of the Christian life in general. The Englishman contends there are two kinds of Christian life: active and contemplative. Of these, the contemplative is higher. Also, there are two degrees of active Christian life – a higher and a lower, and two degrees of contemplative Christian life – a higher and a lower. Active life begins and ends on earth. The contemplative life will extend into eternity, because the contemplative life is "Mary's part which shall never be taken away. The active life is troubled and busy about many things but the contemplative life *sits in peace with the one necessary thing.*"[48]

The *lower active life* is comprised of busying oneself with good deeds and works of mercy. Because the *higher active life* and the *lower contemplative life* flow into each other, they

---

[47] Ibid., 72-73.
[48] Ibid., 58. Here the Englishman refers to the gospel account of Mary and Martha, of Luke 10:38-42.

are to a great degree functionally synonymous, and consist of thanking God for His works in creation, and beginning to meditate on the things of the Spirit, human sinfulness, Christ's Passion, and other Christian fundamentals. While yet earthbound, the *higher contemplative life* entails encounters with darkness and the cloud of unknowing as God is pursued with love and desire. In this schemata, the relevant point the Englishman would have us remember is that because the higher contemplative life is a *work*, it should not be left behind in order to pursue the lower order of works. It is the lower order which must, at least during the specific work of contemplative prayer, be left behind.[49]

Even with the above, *The Cloud* author recognizes that there exists something of a process in the assumption of these various levels of Christian life. Christians typically grow into these levels in four phases: Common, Special, Singular, and Perfect. The first three may be begun and completed on earth, whereas the last may be begun here, but will only be completed in the hereafter.[50] In the Common phase, Christians go about their day-to-day mundane existence, in the company of their friends. The Special phase is marked by God calling the individual out from amongst His sheep, to be His special friend, in the company of His friends; 'the interior life' is lived more perfectly. Those of the Singular phase live at the deep, solitary core of their being, directing their love and desire toward "the highest and final manner of living,"[51] which is called Perfect. The Perfect phase involves ongoing, unencumbered intimacy with God.

---

[49] Ibid., 58-59.
[50] Ibid., 45.
[51] Ibid., 46

Practical Benefits of Contemplation

Also in response to critics, the superiority of contemplation can be demonstrated in very practical applications. For example, humility, a queen of the virtues, like all other virtues is only perfect when God is its source. The contemplative work of love stands far above all other possible works in regard to the generation of God-given humility, because:

> the secret love of a pure heart pressing upon the dark cloud of unknowing between you and your God in a hidden yet certain way includes in itself perfect humility without the help of particular or clear ideas.[52]

In other words, the sheer, voluntary dependence on God and His mercy necessary in such a vulnerable, wanting position, "includes in itself perfect humility." Contrariwise, if "particular or clear ideas" (or any other created thing, for that matter) were to help-out in this situation, the dependence on God would of necessity decrease.

The practicality of contemplation is also evident in its supporting the fulfillment of both the primary and secondary Christian commandments – loving God and loving neighbor. "In real charity one loves God for himself alone above every created thing and he loves his fellow man because it is God's law."[53] By its very essence, contemplative prayer fulfills the foremost commandment, in that, "Wholly intent upon God, this simple love beats unceasingly upon the dark cloud of unknowing."[54] The secondary command is also fulfilled, though

---

[52] Ibid., 67.
[53] Ibid., 80.
[54] Ibid.

differently. During the actual time of prayer, "the skilled contemplative has no special regard for any person in particular," but the *result* of such prayer is a disposition in which "no man is a stranger... because he looks on each one as a brother."[55] All persons are treated as best friends.

In any case, the Englishman suggests that those who criticize contemplation do so only because they have not experienced it. In light of this, he admonishes his disciples to avoid defending themselves from the at-

> **The Englishman suggests that those who criticize contemplation do so only because they have not experienced it.**

tacks of the worldly or activity-minded. They should be so occupied with their work that they do not notice such attacks.[56] As He did with Mary, Jesus will surely defend those who spend their time nestled at His feet. If contemplatives do reply to 'active' critics, it should be confined to the words of the Lord, "Martha, Martha..."[57]

Controlling Unwanted Thoughts

Regarding the inevitable thoughts which arise in the mind while practicing contemplative prayer, the Englishman suggests combating them with the phrase "God alone I seek and desire, only him."[58] If those thoughts in turn ask, "Who is this God?" tell them He is "the one who created you, redeemed you, and brought you to this work. Say to your thoughts, 'You

---

[55] Ibid., 80-81.
[56] Ibid., 74.
[57] Ibid., 77. Once again, a reference to the 'Mary and Martha' account of Luke 10.
[58] Ibid., 55.

are powerless to grasp him. Be still.' "[59] Seekers must not be distracted, even by what may seem to be worthy thoughts.

Alternately, *The Cloud* author suggests using a sacred word. The word, preferably monosyllabic, is to be used as a club to vanquish competing thoughts or arguments which would otherwise draw the seeker away from the goal of naked love toward God.[60] 'Sin' or 'God' are to be preferred, as these words encapsulate the work of the contemplative. Sin, because it reveals the seekers' desire to do away with evil; and God, because it reveals the seekers' desire for Him. These two little words express all which is either good or evil.[61]

---

[59] Ibid.
[60] Ibid., 56.
[61] Ibid., 98.

CHAPTER TWO

THE ROLE OF REASON
IN *THE CLOUD OF UNKNOWING*

HISTORICAL RENDERINGS OF REASON
IN CHRISTIAN MYSTICISM

Though there have always been mystics in the Christian church, they have often been viewed with suspicion. This suspicion and subsequent reproach has largely resulted from the idea that mysticism is vague, vast, sentimental, and without factual or logical basis. Hence, the role of reason (communicable mental processes of interacting with concepts) in Christian mysticism has consistently been scrutinized and debated. Should reason prevail? Or should the mysterious, ineffable, spiritual aspects of the faith take precedent?

As this relationship is considered, it is important to note that it has frequently been couched in variant terms: faith versus reason, or understanding versus belief. The role of reason in mysticism might well be counted a subset of these categories, in that mysticism is commonly conceived as a particular, radical expression of faith/belief. In any case, historical positions generally fall into one of two camps: 1) one must understand in order to believe, or 2) one must believe in order to understand.

As the explicitly biblical view of this relationship will be taken-up in chapter four, the current inquiry will begin with the church fathers.

Ideas of faith versus reason in the church fathers were in great measure formulated in response to interaction with Greek philosophy. Some fathers viewed philosophy as an adversary, others assumed it as a tool. As these positions took shape, the juxtaposition involved the 'faith' procured by special revelation and the 'reason' represented by philosophy. For Tertullian, pagan philosophy was little more than worldly foolishness. Clement of Alexandria viewed philosophy as a gift from God. Both Clement and Justin Martyr believed that Plato had received much of his wisdom from Moses and the other Hebrew prophets, and that accordingly, significant elements of Greek philosophy could both be integrated into Christian thinking and used as an in-road to evangelizing intellectuals.[62]

Of these positions, it was that of Clement and Justin which won-out amongst the fathers, at least as represented by that patristic capstone and medieval foundation stone – Aurelius Augustinus.

Ironically, however, a man instrumental in bringing Augustine to faith in Christ, Ambrose, the late fourth century bishop of Milan, had little respect for reason as an instrument of religious knowledge. "You are commanded to believe," he wrote, "not permitted to inquire... To Abraham it was counted as righteousness that he sought no reasons but believed with most ready faith. It seemed good that faith should go before reason, lest we seem to exact a reason from our Lord God as

---

[62] Frederick Copleston, *A History of Philosophy*, vol. 2, *Medieval Philosophy* (New York: Doubleday, 1993), 15.

from a man... By faith we come to knowledge, and by knowledge to discipline."[63]

As for Ambrose's disciple, Augustine himself, the issue was more complex than is generally believed. While Augustine is oft represented as propagating the *fides proecedit intelligam*[64] motif, and rightly so, his employment of that notion must be contextualized to be properly understood. As brought out by Lewis, in many instances faith did precede reason, while in other instances, reason preceded faith.[65] On the whole, Augustine believed reason precedes faith in ascertaining *what* to believe and *why* to believe, concerning temporal things (*scientia*), including the biblical record. Rationally verified biblical accounts, their correlative propositions, and the realities to which they conform, including those of the resurrected and living Christ, were then 'believed.' Subsequent to exercising saving faith, Augustine asserted that further knowledge of eternal things (*sapientia*), including God's redemptive program, was attained primarily by faith as opposed to intellect. It is through the mediation of faith that a regenerate mind becomes illumined to biblical principles.[66]

Said to be of the Augustinian tradition, the great eleventh century bishop of Canterbury, Anselm, actually had a unique approach to the issue, which is severally at odds with Augustine. While personalizing Augustine's motif in the form of *credo ut intelligam,*[67] Anselm seemed to use it in the opposite

---

[63] Avery Dulles, *A History of Apologetics* (New York: Corpus Instrumentorum, 1971), 50.

[64] Latin for "faith precedes reason."

[65] Gordon R. Lewis, "Faith and History in St. Augustine," *Trinity Journal* 3 (NS 1982), 40-41.

[66] Ibid., 40-41, 49-50.

[67] Latin: "I believe that I might understand."

manner. For Anselm, to do theology was to "move from faith
to understanding... to understand is nothing other than to grasp
the objective reasons, the *rationes*, that underlie and illumine
the data of faith."[68] That is, while moved into the arena of
understanding through the regenerative power of God through
faith, understanding is then pursued through rationality only.
This approach was demonstrated by Anselm in his three major
writings. He wrote them in such a way that one fully unfamil-
iar with Scripture (an object of and springboard to faith) could
apprehend them (solely through reason).

Peter Abelard tended toward a supporting role for reason,
in which reason "paves the way for the supernatural act of faith
elicited under the influence of grace and charity."[69] He argued
against a blind faith, stating that faith such as Abraham's is an
exceptional work of grace, and not normative for Christians.
Rational assessment of data prior to *assensus*[70] is the rule.

The eminent scholastic, Thomas Aquinas, taught that
some truths are beyond the reach of reason, being attainable
only through revelation or mysticism. Or as Copleston inter-
prets him, "Man was created for a profounder and more intimate knowledge of God than he can attain by the exercise of
his natural reason in this life."[71] Thus, special revelation was
necessary. While natural reason can stretch to encompass
much of that which naturally surrounds humanity, something
higher than reason is needed both to compel and enable humanity to "zealously strive towards something 'which exceeds

---

[68] Dulles, *Apologetics*, 77.
[69] Ibid., 83.
[70] Latin: "affirmation."
[71] Copleston, *Philosophy*, 310.

the whole state of this life.' "[72] Just as the philosophical discipline of metaphysics has an object of its own (to understand being, that which is), it at the same time "points upwards and needs to be crowned by theology."[73] Accordingly, "God exceeds the apprehension of the metaphysician and of the natural reason in general, and as the full knowledge or vision of God is not attainable in this life, the conceptual knowledge of God is crowned in this life by mysticism."[74]

Julian of Norwich, a contemporary of *The Cloud* author, profited from the empirical/natural approach to philosophy that Aquinas forwarded. But he also came to experience that crown of conceptual knowledge – mysticism – in a personal revelation from God. Julian was shown "everything that is made," as a little thing lying in his hand. And from this, God revealed to him that "all things have their being by the grace of God," in that they exist and shall ever exist because God made them, God loves them, and God keeps them.[75]

The Reformers in general held that religious faith was of a multifaceted character, consisting of: *noticia*, the content of Christian faith, those data which are to be believed; *assensus*, intellectual ascent to the truth of those data; and *fiducia*, the personal dimension of trust without which one cannot be counted a Christian.[76] *Fiducia* amounts to placing one's life in the hands of that which or He who is trusted. Considering

---

[72] Ibid., 310-311.
[73] Ibid., 311.
[74] Ibid., 311.
[75] William Dyrness, *Christian Apologetics in a World Community* (Downers Grove: Inter-Varsity Press, 1983), 34.
[76] R. C. Sproul, John Gerstner and Arthur Lindsley, *Classical Apologetics* (Grand Rapids: Zondervan Publishing House, 1984), 21-22.

the faith versus reason question, then, reason is most prominent in the first two stages, but is superseded by intuitive and volitional elements in the third.

A voice critical of philosophy, highlighting its tendencies toward contradiction and inconclusiveness, was Blaise Pascal. Concerning the wrestling of philosophy and her handmaid, reason, over the nature of the soul, Pascal mocks, "If Reason is reasonable, then she will be reasonable enough to admit she has failed to discover anything significant."[77] Reason, he says, is dependent upon heart/instinct for all its arguments, because it is from the intuitive knowledge of "first principles, like space, time, motion, and number," that subsequent arguments from reason must be based.[78] "Principles are known by intuition, whereas propositions are inferred, yet all with certainty though in differing ways."[79]

For Leibniz, faith is in a certain sense above reason, but never contrary to it. Faith should not be blind or irrational. The "truths of faith necessarily agree with the *a priori*[80] principles of reason, such as the principle of contradiction and the principle of sufficient reason."[81]

Turning the page to the modern age, William James offers that of all which humanity considers mentally, only a small portion can be accounted for rationally. And though rational notions are those which normally possess prestige (per modernity), rationality nevertheless, fails miserably if asked to overcome conclusions arrived at through intuition, as intuitive data

[77] Blaise Pascal, *Mind on Fire*, ed. James M. Houston (Minneapolis: Bethany House Publishers, 1997), 108.
[78] Ibid., 84-85.
[79] Ibid., 85.
[80] Latin: "first."
[81] Dulles, *Apologetics*, 147.

seems to possess a depth foreign to rationalism. Thus, it is intuition, not rationality, upon which the deepest beliefs, needs, and premises are based. "This inferiority of the rationalist level in founding belief is just as manifest when rationalism argues for religion as when it argues against it."[82]

In speaking of the genuinely mysterious nature of aspects of the Christian faith, particularly those given by special revelation, C. Stephen Evans says, "The basic mysteries of the faith are *above* reason, but not *against* reason. That is, although we cannot fully understand them or prove their truth, they do not contradict what *is* known to be truth."[83]

Though admittedly not a Christian, in his book on the metaphysically necessary nature of reason, Thomas Nagle provides insightful comments on the common but diverse roles which reason and intuition play in human engagement with reality: "Reason provides regulative methods and principles, and perception and intuition provide reason with the initial material to work on... We constantly move from appearance to reality in this way."[84] In this scenario, raw material would be supplied by perceptive, intuitive experience, which would then be subject to the scrutiny of reason.

It may be concluded that though positions vary in history's Great Conversation, Nagle's conclusion is generally acknowledged: reason is typically conceived as a regulative faculty which may direct intuitive and mystical activities and/or assess the raw material gathered by those activities.

---

[82] William James, *Varieties of Religious Experience* (New York: Longmans, Green, and Co., 1928), 73.
[83] Douglas R. Groothuis, *Confronting the New Age* (Downers Grove IL: InterVarsity Press, 1988), 76.
[84] Thomas Nagel, *The Last Word* (New York: Oxford University Press, 1997), 16.

REASON'S UTILITY IN *THE CLOUD*

The Cloud author warns his readers that if they read any portion of his manuscript, they are to read the whole thing. Reading only a portion may result in misunderstanding due to failure to sufficiently consider the context of that portion.[85] By implication, the author is concerned not only with error, but its opposite – truth. And truth is,

> **The Cloud author is concerned not only with error, but its opposite – truth... And contemplative prayer is to an extent, dependent upon rationality.**

at least minimally, a function of reason. Hence, the Englishman exhibits a concern for reason. The nature of the error the author is concerned with also indicates something of the extent to which reason applies in this situation. That is, if the reader misunderstands a pericope, it will be due to miscontextualization; and miscontextualization and its converse, contextualization, is a function of reason, as in correlating, inferring, deducing, and so forth. Further, the Englishman is concerned that misunderstandings of a given pericope will result in subsequent misapplications of his counsel. This implies that contemplative prayer is to an extent, dependent upon rationality, at least as rationality functions in giving, receiving, and applying instruction.

In another place, *The Cloud* author explicitly insists that reason be employed prior to contemplation. He advocates three specific disciplines to all aspiring contemplatives: study/reading, reflection/thinking, and prayer. Seekers cannot

---

[85] Johnston, *The Cloud*, 46.

properly pray apart from familiarity with the word of God; and they cannot be familiar with the word of God without study/reading; but if they cannot read, they must at least listen to others who have read, and reflect upon their words. "God's Word, written or spoken, is like a mirror. Reason is your spiritual eye and conscience your spiritual reflection."[86] Anyone wishing to see clearly and discern rightly must utilize reason. Reason also aids the conscience in assessing one's spiritual condition.

The significant place the Englishman allocates to reason, though atypical for mystics, particularly those of a monistic disposition (as will be more fully explored in chapter three), should not be surprising coming from a Christian. In a fascinating chapter, the author theologizes on the hierarchical relationship of created things. Humans, he says, stand above all created things, including splendid things such as the stars, sun and moon. Our only equals in nature, as intelligent creatures, are other humans and angels. Humans are gifted by nature "with three marvelous spiritual faculties, Mind, Reason, and Will, and two secondary faculties, Imagination and Feeling. There is nothing above you in nature except God himself."[87]

That the Englishman counts Mind and Reason as spiritual faculties, and Imagination and Feeling as but secondary faculties, is significant in its opposition to many mystical traditions. As for their more exact functions, he says:

> Reason, Will, Imagination, and Feeling are man's vital working powers through which he processes the data of reality. Mind is the comprehensive faculty which receives,

---

[86] Ibid., 92-93.
[87] Ibid., 129.

sorts, and retains the knowledge acquired through the other four faculties.[88]

Here the Mind, as the comprehensive faculty, functions similarly to Nagle's 'reason,' in that it does not so much acquire data as it 'understands' the data acquired through the other faculties.

Primary faculties are distinguished from secondary faculties not because man's spirit is divisible, but because the data processed are divisible into two main categories. The primary faculties engage data related to spirit, whereas the secondary engage those related to matter. Because Reason and Will "deal directly with spiritual things, they can function independently of Imagination and Feeling."[89] Imagination and Feeling deal with material things because "they reside in the body and function through the medium of the body's five senses."[90] While Reason and Will function honestly, "Imagination and Feeling require the assistance of Reason and Will in order to grasp even material things in their entirety."[91] Feeling and Imagination are unable to access material things independent of the primary faculties.

The Cloud author's regard for reason is also exemplified in his frequent references to specific theological data: the fall, the incarnation, God's redeeming grace, the centrality of

> *The Cloud* **author's regard for reason is also exemplified in his frequent references to specific theological data.**

Christ, and Christ's deity. He even admits that it is good to

---

[88] Ibid., 130.
[89] Ibid., 131.
[90] Ibid.
[91] Ibid.

ponder God's attributes and deeds for the insight such can yield, though he counsels against doing so in the midst of contemplation. There are propositional elements, however, which can carry-over directly into contemplative prayer; namely, identifying the God you are seeking: He is the God who created you, redeemed you, and is guiding you to this work.[92] Even so, such identifying procedures are to be marginally employed in the work of contemplation. As previously noted, the Englishman views it superior to simply move with a naked intent toward God.

The last but crucial function of reason which will here be highlighted within *The Cloud*'s mysticism is: "Remember that the nearer a man comes to the truth the more sensitive he must become to error."[93] If truth is to be discerned and distinguished from error, such must at least include propositions about reality and the

> "...the nearer a man comes to the truth the more sensitive he must become to error."

correspondence of those propositions to reality, in other words, a rational process.

REASON'S LIMITS IN *THE CLOUD*

In a wide departure from typical conceptions of mystical works, *The Cloud* author presents his readers with a sophisticated theology of the role of reason in humanity:

Reason is the faculty which enables us to distinguish the bad

---

[92] Ibid., 55-56.
[93] Ibid., 91.

from the good, the good from the better, and the better from
the best... Before man sinned he did this naturally and easily
but now Reason, blinded as a consequence of original sin,
errs unless it is illumined by grace.[94]

Reason does have a primary role in human experience, but the
efficacy of that role immediately decreased as a result of sin.
While reason once went about its task of discernment without
qualification or impediment, the rational capacity of fallen humans diminished. Left to its own, reason is now prone to mis-
leading its subjects.

But does the Englishman lend any insight as to the *modus
operandi*[95] of reason? And how does it interface with the other
'spiritual faculties' of Mind and Will? "The Mind embraces
both Reason and its object. After Reason has determined what
is good, the Will moves toward it with love and desire and
finally rests in it with satisfaction, delight, and full consent."[96]

Mind is something of a container in which Reason and
Will exist. Reason, being the ever ready discernment faculty,
makes its judgment as to what is good. Will then pursues the
identified good.

What must follow from such a dynamic, affected by such
a history, is the inevitable debilitation of human choices and
action. So *The Cloud* author concludes:

Before original sin, man was in no danger of choosing and
loving a false good because in his primordial integrity he
experienced each thing as it really was. All his faculties
were sound and he was not liable to be deceived by any of
them. But in the present order of things, man cannot con-

---

[94] Ibid., 131.
[95] Latin: "mode of operation."
[96] Johnston, *The Cloud*, 131.

sistently choose the good without the assistance of grace. Original sin left him wounded and blind so that he is easily deceived by appearances and chooses an evil which has disguised itself as good.[97]

This theological backdrop largely orders the Englishman's mystical approach. Though reason has a role in the path to God, that role must be tempered by virtue of reason becoming skewed by sin.

Thus, in contemplation *The Cloud* stresses the role of the will ("naked *intent*") and love rather than reason. Given its current susceptibility to being deceived, at choosing evil disguised as good, reason must at a certain point be sloughed off. But such a tactic seems problematic: If will is directed by reason, and reason can no longer be trusted in its directing toward good, how can will be trusted in an untempered march toward God? How can seekers be sure their will is marching toward God, and not some impostor? Though the Englishman never identifies this particular problem, it could be argued that he nevertheless answers it, at least in part: "A man may know completely and ponder thoroughly every created thing and its works, yes, and God's works, too, but not God himself. Thought cannot comprehend God."[98] The author makes a distinction between knowing *created things* in a complete and thorough way via reason – it is possible, and knowing God in a similar way – it is not possible. God's uniqueness as Creator, and in the infinitude of His other attributes, puts Him out of the finite reach of human intellect. The Englishman could ar-

---

[97] Ibid.
[98] Ibid., 54.

gue, therefore (though he does not in the text), that the thorough knowledge of created things available to humans allows seekers to place those created things beneath them under the cloud of forgetting. The only thing remaining for the will to pursue would be the uncreated God.

But even this argument is not without difficulty, as to conject a 'complete' knowledge of virtually anything, created or not, seems unfounded. How thoroughly, for example, do humans know electricity, atoms, or angels?

Continuing to follow the Englishman's argument, it must be asked that if reason is up to the task of steering seekers in the proper direction, is it then to be abandoned at a certain point? From the utility of reason in *The Cloud*, explored above, it can be concluded that the Englishman *expects* reason to be employed in preparation for contemplation. Such preparation was to include study/reading, reflection/thinking, and prayer. It follows that the directive power of reason is to be utilized to get seekers on the right contemplative path. That is, through discreet study/reading, reflection/thinking, and prayer, reason can guide the seeker to the path toward the only true God, a path which corresponds with biblical revelation. Reason can be trusted to get the seeker this far. But as Walsh suggests, unlike Pseudo-Dionysius and Thomas Aquinas, the Englishman does not think it necessary "for the mind to go to the limit of what it can do to approach the mystery before admitting defeat."[99] Though all three giants admit the limits of intellect to this end, the older two would retain the faculty as far into orbit as they could, while the younger would jettison it shortly after launch.

---

[99] James S. J. Walsh, ed., *The Cloud of Unknowing* (New York: Paulist Press, 1981), xiv.

As an overall strategy, however, the Englishman agrees with both Pseudo-Dionysius and Aquinas in his quest for intimacy with God. Both of the ancients said there are two ways man can know God: one is the way of reason (λογος),[100] the other is the way of mystical contemplation (μυστικον θεαμα).[101] Theology and philosophy comprise both the means to and store of rational knowledge of God, while a superior intuitive, ineffable knowledge can be had through mysticism.[102] Though the 'hidden' knowledge of mysticism is counted as superior by all three, they do not deny that discursive reason can yield informative, directive data.

Dionysius famously added that there are even two ways of knowing God by reason: one affirmative, the other negative. Whereas theology and philosophy normally adhere to the former, Dionysius' unique contribution was the latter, the *via negativa*:[103] "That most divine knowledge of God which takes place by ignorance."[104] But where Dionysius leaves it at that, *The Cloud* author takes it up with one of his unique contributions: love. God can ultimately be embraced only by love. Neither humans nor angels can grasp him by knowledge, "For the intellect of both men and angels is too small to comprehend God as he is in himself."[105] Though rational creatures possess both a knowing power and a loving power, the uncreated God cannot be fully comprehended with knowledge. It is only

---

[100] Greek term transliterated *logos*, and translated as *word*, *reason*, or *revelation*.
[101] Greek term transliterated *mystikon theama*.
[102] Johnston, *The Cloud*, 25.
[103] Latin: "negative way."
[104] Johnston, *The Cloud*, 25.
[105] Ibid., 50.

through love that He can be fully grasped. "So," the Englishman says, "I prefer to abandon all I can know, choosing rather
to love him whom I cannot know."[106]

"For however much a man may know about every created
spiritual thing," he continues, "his intellect will never be able
to comprehend the uncreated spiritual truth which is God."[107]
In effect, the Englishman is saying that God, unlike other
truths, stands outside the scope of propositions. Though God
might be predicated by 'love,' 'spirit' and 'truth' in Scripture,
the infinite nature of those predicates when applied to God
place them outside the scope of human comprehension. Thus,
it is best, the author concludes, to lay such efforts aside in the
quest to embrace the deity.

This same suprarational phenomenon is well expressed by
The Cloud author not only in the pursuit of God, but in the
finding of Him. In those rare and precious moments, the contemplative can expect God to "touch you with a ray of his divine light which will pierce the cloud of unknowing between
you and him. He will let you glimpse something of the ineffable secrets of his divine wisdom and your affection will seem
on fire with his love. I am at a loss to say more, for the experience is beyond words... I dare not try to describe God's grace
with my crude and awkward tongue."[108]

---

[106] Ibid., 54.
[107] Ibid., 139.
[108] Ibid., 84.

CONTEXTUALIZING *THE CLOUD*'S
USE OF REASON

In sum, *The Cloud* author's attribution of a significant and necessary role for reason in mystical pursuits is unique regards to mysticism in general, but is not so regarding Christian mysticism.   As noted, most Christians, even

> **Most Christians, even those of a mystical orientation, acknowledge the vital place of reason in their belief system.**

those of a mystical orientation, acknowledge the vital place of reason in their belief system. But such should not be surprising in light of the unique status of Christianity amongst world religions – that it is based not only upon spiritual and axiological drives and concerns, but upon empirically sufficient and logically consistent data. Christianity is a history-based religion. And on the weight of historical evidence pertaining to the likes of the life, death, and resurrection of Jesus Christ, claims of spiritual and eternal consequence follow. Reason, then, allows an access to and assessment of those data relevant to a subsequent faith commitment.

As *The Cloud*, however, is concerned not with the data (*noticia*) and reasoning which may lead to faith (*assensus*), but with paths to intimacy with God which follow that faith, such emphases on this type of reasoning are not referenced. He is, after all, a Christian writing to Christians. Accordingly, he apparently makes certain assumptions: that his pupils are sufficiently cognizant of the data of faith and have lent their personal assent to that data; and that they are actively trusting (*fiducia*) in the object of that faith – the triune God of the Bible – which has resulted in their salvation.

Reason in *The Cloud*, then, has primarily to do with its role in post-salvation pursuit of encounter with Yehovah, and this particular pursuit is *The Cloud*'s idea of Christian mysticism.[109] With this understanding in tow, the Englishman does acknowledge that reason can, even in the midst of contemplative prayer, help seekers remain focused on which God they are pursuing, as well as what He is like, and how He may best be encountered. And while the rational propositions of Scripture reveal something of the nature and character of God, those propositions themselves are not God. Though a person can know *about* God through the Bible, relationally *knowing* and communing with God Himself requires something more. And whereas that relationship and communion is initiated in the regenerative act of salvation, as is a love for God, these very facets of personal interaction birthed within Christians by God reaching down to them in the incarnation of Jesus Christ and in the person of the Holy Spirit, *should* generate within Christians a desire to reciprocate – to reach out toward God in an effort to enhance that relationship. And one way to do this, per *The Cloud*, is through contemplative prayer.

> ...while the rational propositions of Scripture reveal something of the nature and character of God, those propositions themselves are not God.

---

[109] It must be acknowledged that mystical encounters with Yehovah are not confined to a post-salvation time-frame. They may also precede and/or accompany the salvation experience. See "Existential Insights" of chapter four for examples of this type.

EVALUATING *THE CLOUD*'S USE OF REASON

Even with the above contextualization, several problematic uses and limits of reason in *The Cloud* remain. Whereas most would admit that human rational capacities do have their limits in relating to One who rises so far above His creatures, care must nevertheless be exercised in too quickly laying reason aside in pursuit of enhancing that relationship. That *The Cloud* author asserts that God can ultimately be embraced not by intellect, but only by love,[110] seems a misunderstanding of what love, and most particularly, love of God, actually entails. The very Bible which the Englishman counts the study of as necessary preparation for contemplative prayer, indicates that proper and complete love of God includes loving Him with all our *mind*.[111] Though God and possibly everything else (e.g., atoms, porpoises) stand outside human ability to *fully* comprehend, this does not mean that those things we can know of God and other objects should be abandoned in an effort to 'truly' know them through some suprarational, mystical means. Both positive and negative assertions about God in Holy Writ serve to enlighten us about who God is: we know that He is loving, holy, and just, and that He is not gold, stone, or the cosmos. Additionally, a Holy Spirit illumined reading of Scripture goes a long way toward revealing the very personality of God, as He reveals how He loves His people, pursues His people, and even chastises His people when necessary; we discover something of how the persons of the Trinity relate to each other; God tells us how He feels when His people are hurt by others,

---

[110] Johnson, *The Cloud*, 54, etc.
[111] Mark 12:30.

as well as how He longingly stands over His people with hopes to soon embrace them. Though Scriptural predicates of God do surpass complete human comprehension by virtue of their infinite nature when applied to God, they are nevertheless true, insofar as they correspond to their referent.

The supernaturally inspired assertions of Scripture enable us to know God more fully than intuition, general revelation, or mystical encounters alone. It is only as Christians come to recognize and utilize the unique contributions of both reason and ordinate mysticism in outreach to God that their efforts will be most fruitful.

> **The supernaturally inspired assertions of Scripture enable us to know God more fully than intuition, general revelation, or mystical encounters alone.**

CHAPTER THREE

THE CLOUD'S RELATION
TO OTHER MYSTICAL EXPRESSIONS

William James, one of the first modern scholars of mysticism, insists that "religious experience has it roots and center in mystical states of consciousness."[112] This is difficult to deny. At a minimum, the power of the statement bespeaks the import of mysticism and its impact upon religions and societies. But what exactly is mysticism? How do mystical experiences of adherents of different religions compare? And how does the Christian mysticism of *The Cloud* fit into the larger picture?

COMMONALITIES WITHIN MYSTICISM

Despite dissimilitudes in time, space, and culture, there remain unitive aspects to mystical experiences. Similar expressions, images, and comparisons exist within mystic literary works whose authors are generally unknown to each other.[113] Intuition leads mystics to believe they have to some

---

[112] James, *Religious Experience*, 379.
[113] Earl Barrett, *A Christian Perspective of Knowing* (Kansas City MO: Beacon Hill Press, 1965), 156.

degree experienced the Ultimate, and if Ultimate, is it not common? The perception of the common results of mysticism are amplified by what is perceived to be the compelling, complete, and self-validating nature of these intuitive insights.

Perhaps the most concise and comprehensive definition of mysticism is offered by Winfried Corduan: "An unmediated link to an absolute."[114] That mysticism can be defined at all, attests to a sameness. But as Corduan's definition stretches, through generalization, to take in the whole phenomenon, James narrows the field somewhat, pointing to four marks which characterize *virtually* all mystical forms: 1) ineffability (they defy expression), 2) noetic quality (states of insight extend beyond discursive intellect), 3) transiency (they are of limited duration), and 4) passivity (personal will is laid aside or overcome).[115]

From the above, it follows that mystics or budding mystics believe there is an absolute, and that they can experience an unmediated link to that absolute via a suprarational encounter. Primacy is attached to such inner spiritual experiences, and to being in the presence of a Reality which surpasses ordinary perceptive processes, including that of reason.

The marks of unity in mysticism are amplified in the

---

[114] Winfried Corduan, *Mysticism: An Evangelical Option?* (Grand Rapids: Zondervan Publishing House, 1991), 41.

[115] James, *Religious Experience*, 380-381.

thoughts of many. In his novel pursuit of mystical experiences associated with the drug culture of the 1960s, journalist William Braden concluded that it is difficult if not impossible to distinguish religious mystical experiences from those induced by LSD or other psychedelic agents. The best known of numerous studies in this vein was undertaken by Harvard's Walter Pahnke. Using the typology of religious mysticism established by the work of W. T. Stace, Pahnke found that ninety percent of a control group of theology students reported having such experiences subsequent to ingesting psilocybin.[116] In another study, literature students exposed to first-hand accounts of both religious mystical and psychedelic experiences, could not distinguish the source or nature of those experiences by virtue of the accounts themselves.[117]

Ideas of a mystical touch with a common Reality are buttressed by recent advances toward religious syncretism. In contemporary Western society, classical Christian constructs are progressively being encroached upon by Easternism. Ever so subtly, and in an array of venues, Christian dualism is being replaced by monism, and the personal deity is being replaced by the impersonal Force. The power behind such trends derives, obviously, from traditional eastern religions, but also from 'progressive' philosophies birthed in academic think tanks which represent themselves as responding to "a need to promote a new image of humanity that will facilitate social transformation."[118] In this train of thinking, old, exclusivist,

---

[116] William Braden, *The Private Sea: LSD and the Search for God* (Chicago: Quadrangle Books, 1967), 38.

[117] Ibid., 39.

[118] B. Alexander, "Occult Philosophy and Mystical Experience," *SCP Journal* 6 (winter 1984), 14.

"insufficient" worldviews (most markedly, theistic and Christian) must be deposed, and replaced by the "the highest common factor in all theologies."[119] Those commonalities are held to be the mystical writings displayed in all religions. Such commonalities, they say, represent the unvarying kernel of truth in humanity's interaction with Reality.

In his *Doors of Perception*, Aldous Huxley reiterates the case for the sameness of mystical experiences. By excerpting quotations from various mystics, he says that regardless of impetus, form, or worldview, they all seem to be saying the same thing.[120]

MYSTICAL COMMONALITIES AND *THE CLOUD*

While argument will be given below that Huxley's conclusion, and those similar, are mistaken, the question remains as to how *The Cloud* corresponds with other mystical forms. As per Corduan, *The Cloud* author is clearly moved by faith to believe that seekers can establish "an unmediated link to an absolute." This is what makes contemplative prayer, by definition, 'mystical.' The Englishman concurs with the primacy attached to such inner experiences, equating them to the "more excellent and necessary" path which Mary chose in relation to Jesus. Inner works in reaching upward to God surpass outward and 'active' works.

As for James' four categories, the Englishman concurs that the phenomenon is predominantly *ineffable* – if and when

---

[119] Ibid.
[120] John P. Newport, *The New Age Movement and the Biblical Worldview* (Grand Rapids: Eerdmans, 1998), 99-100.

'contact' with God occurs.[121] However, external, verbal expressions to God must not be prohibited in mystical enterprises. It is erroneous to unduly separate body and spirit, particularly in light of the fact that God united them. Just as the
whole person is to join Him in eternity, contemplatives should
honor Him with their whole person now, including their
mouth/speech.[122]

The Cloud author says little of the *noetic quality* which
may or may not inhere in contemplative prayer, except for one
reference to the high point of such prayer – when God allows
the prayer to break through the cloud of unknowing: "He will
let you glimpse something of the ineffable secrets of his divine
wisdom and your affection will seem on fire with his love."[123]
Clearly, to glimpse 'something of His divine wisdom,' implies
at least some content in the experience, albeit an ineffable, suprarational content.

Regarding *transiency*, it is certain that the 'high point' of
contemplation is predominantly fleeting and infrequent, at
least for most folks. These "can-
not reach it without long and frequent spiritual exercises; and
even then it is only very seldom
that they will experience the perfection of this exercise, at the spe-

> There are those...
> who have a rare
> ability to tap into
> 'the presence'
> nearly at whim.

cial calling of the Lord."[124] Tapping into 'the presence' depends both on the "spiritual capacity" of the seeker and "the

---

[121] Johnston, *The Cloud*, 84.
[122] Ibid., 109.
[123] Ibid., 84.
[124] Walsh, *The Cloud*, 257.

ordinance and disposition of God."[125] But there are those, the Englishman admits, who have a rare ability to tap into 'the presence' nearly at whim. These:

> are so refined by grace and in spirit, and so familiar with God in this grace of contemplation, that they may have the perfection of it whenever they will, in their ordinary state of soul: whether they are sitting, walking, standing or kneeling.[126]

Such proficiency and constancy in Christian mystical enterprise presages the likes of Brother Lawrence and Frank Laubach, and their famed *Practice of the Presence of God*.[127]

The *passivity* of contemplative work, as prescribed by *The Cloud*, is in many ways in full contrast to James' laying aside of the personal will, in that the heart of contemplative prayer is 'a naked intent,' an unrelenting will toward God. Even if everything else is laid aside – creatures, thoughts – will is not. Whether placing all created things under 'the cloud of forgetting,' or pressing up toward 'the cloud of unknowing,' the contemplative's will must be active.

DISTINCTIONS OF MYSTIC FORMS

Given the fact that there are commonalities to mysticism, does it follow that it is a unified phenomenon? No. The wide divides between mystic forms are perhaps most apparent in

---

[125] Ibid.

[126] Ibid., 258.

[127] Brother Lawrence and Frank Laubach, *Practicing His Presence* (Beaumont, TX: The SeedSowers, 1973).

worldviews. As mystics represent virtually all world religions and even non-religionists, the views which are carried into mystic endeavors are just as varied. Though mysticism takes many forms: Eastern, Western, philosophical, religious, contemplative, practical, positive, negative, introvert, extrovert, ethical intuitionism, radical empiricism, mystical intuitionism, and mystical idealism,[128] those which exhibit the greatest divergence are represented by the worldviews of theism and pantheistic monism. While atheism is certainly more antithetical to theism than is pantheism, few atheists are religionists or mystics.

The theist-pantheist divide comes into play at numerous junctures. In his exposé of Transcendental Meditation (a monistic, Hinduistic implant in the West), Gordon Lewis points out,

> The ultimate goal of a meditator is not freedom from stress, happiness or additional creativity. It is, like a yogi, to lose his individuality in pure Being... Since this state is beyond all differentiation nothing can be said about it. The best one can do is repeat, "I am That, You are That and all this is That."[129]

As Transcendental Meditation could well be understood as a mystical practice, it is apparent that monist aims in mysticism involve metaphysical union with the impersonal, pervasive Constituent of the universe, variously described as That, One, or Brahman. Such a union necessarily includes the dissolution

---

[128] Barrett, *Perspective of Knowing*, 155.
[129] Gordon R. Lewis, *What Everyone Should Know About Transcendental Meditation* (Glendale CA: G/L Regal Books, 1975), 39.

of the individuality, personality, consciousness, and agency of the parties involved. Pantheistic mystical practice also gives rise to epistemological monism – the doctrine that in regard to knowing, subject and object, percept and concept are indistinct – thus, truth and error become indistinguishable.

In contrast, theistic concepts of mysticism generally do not entail absorption into the Ultimate, but a voluntary, non-metaphysical union or communion with a personal God who stands fully distinct from His creation. The personality and individuality of the mystic are maintained. This metaphysical dualism of theism extends itself epistemologically as well: subject and object, percept and concept, truth and error retain their distinctions. Specifically Christian versions of theistic mysticism will be elaborated in the next section.

Along with worldviews, distinctions between mystic traditions are well illustrated by other particular religious phenomena, such as worship and prayer. Just as people from different religious traditions can be said to pray and worship, yet preserve the distinctions of their religions *in* their praying and worship, so it is with mystical engagement.[130]

> **Just as people from different religious traditions can be said to pray and worship, yet preserve the distinctions of their religions *in* their praying and worship, so it is with mystical engagement.**

Distinctions in similar religious activities, including mysticism, manifest when the *object* of those activities, the *methods* of those activities, and the *truth* propositions surrounding those activities are considered.

---

[130] Corduan, *Mysticism*, 59-60.

Mystical experiences also vary per what induces them. Experiences may be spurred, either purposefully or inadvertently by: recitation of phrases, sentences, or passages; dejavu; drugs; exposure to the great outdoors; "cosmic consciousness"; yoga; enlightenment;[131] body movements or postures; solitude; silence; asceticism; prayer; or worship.

Along with union or communion with the Ultimate, mystical states may be accompanied by purported visions, auditions, bi-location, levitation, lights, altered color perception, exhilaration, electrical sensations, sense of expanding or moving upward, vanquishing of fear, roaring sound, wind, separation from physical self, euphoria, awareness of geometric patterns, feelings of liberation, melding of the senses (synthesia), "awakening," transcending time and space, and percepts that the mystical state is real while ordinary consciousness is transitory.[132]

MYSTICAL DISTINCTIONS AND *THE CLOUD*

In all of this, how does *The Cloud* distinguish itself? *The Cloud* author is indisputably a theistic dualist, not a monist. The 'absolute' the Englishman seeks is not That, but Yehovah, the personal God of the Bible. He does not aim at metaphysical union with God (which will be elaborated in chapter five). Advocating the distinguishing of truth from error, he retains epistemological dualism. The Englishman, as mentioned above, does not ascribe to the 'passive' approach identified by James, but a "naked *intent*" toward God. He does not resort to

---

[131] James, *Religious Experience*, 382-404.
[132] James W. Sire, *The Universe Next Door* (Downers Grove, IL: InterVarsity Press, 1997), 155.

narcotics to achieve his ends, vis-à-vis Braden, but to contrite prayer. And though he speaks of the euphoria and exhilaration which accompany successful contemplation, he explicitly distances himself from fanciful or ostentatious manifestations thereof.

But concerning these distinctions, could it not be said – as per James, Braden, and Huxley – that they are just superficial? Could it not be said that underlying the variance in presuppositions surrounding, methodologies toward, and interpretations of mystical experiences, there exists a unifying Reality which is experienced by all mystics, and hence, that the experience itself is common, unified? After all, if an objective reality is distinguished *only* by presuppositions surrounding it, methodologies toward it, and interpretations of it, it *does not* follow that the reality itself is variant. And given the similitude of mystical experiences themselves, as reported by Braden and others, an argument could be made that it *is* a common Reality which is simply being variously approached and interpreted.

While the *possibility* of the sameness of mystical experiences must be acknowledged, a case will be made in chapter four that there are incommensurate distinctions between normative Christian mysticism and normative non-Christian mysticism.

CHRISTIAN MYSTICISM IN HISTORY

Though often vilified in Christian circles, "mysticism experienced in its origins is thoroughly Christian, biblical, sacramental and communitarian."[133] And while many, including

---

[133] Johnston, *Christian Mysticism*, 20.

Reformers, nineteenth century scholars, and Christian contemporaries, have tried to debunk mysticism – both the word and the phenomenon – viewing it as pagan or neoplatonic, such likely results from failure to astutely examine the concept, and the usage of the word in the ancient texts.

Etiologically, 'mysticism' stems from μυεω,[134] in reference to "initiates into the mysteries,"[135] which evolved into μυστηριον,[136] as used by the Greeks in describing their mystery religions. New Testament authors, in turn, adopted the term in speaking of the 'mysteries' of the Christian faith.[137]

These mystic orientations carried over into the subsequent centuries. Origen considered biblical interpretation a religious and mystical experience. Although veering away from Origen's extreme spiritualizing or more rightly, allegorizing of Scripture, Augustine carried on the mystic tradition in the Christian West.[138] Subsequent to him, however, it was not until the twelfth century that mysticism again arose in the West. The fifth century's St. Nilus said that the Eucharist must be

---

[134] Greek term transliterated *myeo.*

[135] Joseph Henry Thayer, *The New Thayer's Greek-English Lexicon of the New Testament* (Peabody, MA: Hendrickson Publishers, 1981), 419.

[136] Greek term transliterated *mysterion.*

[137] Matthew 8:11; Mark 4:11; Luke 8:10; Romans 16:25; 1 Corinthians 2:7; Ephesians 3:9; Colossians 1:26; etc.

[138] Andrew Louth, *The Origins of the Christian Mystical Tradition* (Oxford: Clarendon Press, 1981), 132-158. Though Augustine, as noted in chapter two, certainly recognized the import of *scientia*, pertaining both to what and why to believe, he also recognized the import of encountering God on an individual, personal level. The intensely personal accounts of the spiritual longings and experiences of Augustine, as represented in his *Confessions*, constitute a seminal presentation of post-biblical mystical theology.

considered "not simple bread, but mystical bread."[139] Mysticism and monasticism were closely related in such figures as Anselm, Peter Damian, Bernard of Clairvaux, and Hugo of St. Victor. Scholasticism and mysticism were embraced as two branches of theology, the one being intellectual, formal, and philosophical, and the other being pietistic and didactic of union with God. Some medievals prevailed in both fields, while others tended to specialize. Hugo of St. Victor, Bonaventure, and Aquinas were all strong in both fields; Duns Scotus and Abelard as scholastics only; Bernard in mysticism only.[140] From the twelfth century to the present, mysticism retains a formal place in Roman Catholicism.

As a rule, early reformationists turned away from mysticism, except Luther's retention of certain Eucharistic, Roman Catholic manifestations. The Reformed church was even less favorable to mysticism than was Lutheranism. "Zwingli had no interest in it, Calvin hated it."[141] In the eighteenth century, mysticism was revived through Quietists such as Fenelon, Guyon, the Moravians, and the German mystics.

More recently, mystical elements of the Christian faith have reasserted themselves in the Pentecostal and Charismatic movements. Pentecostalism arose in the first years of the twentieth century as signs and wonders associated with the χαρισματα[142] spoken of in the New Testament[143] manifest

---

[139] Johnston, *Christian Mysticism*, 18.
[140] C. A. Beckwith, "Mysticism," in *The New Schaff-Herzog Encyclopedia of Religious Knowledge*: vol. 8 (Grand Rapid MI: Baker Book House, 1953).
[141] Ibid.
[142] Transliterated *charismata*, Greek for "spiritual gifts."
[143] See 1 Peter 4:10; 1 Corinthians 7:7; 2 Corinthians 1:11; Romans 1:11, 5:15, etc.

amongst a young group of seekers, and quickly spread across America, and shortly thereafter, the world. Whereas Pentecostalism tended to thrive amongst those on the lower end of the socio-economic spectrum, the exuberance of their experiences birthed desires for similar touches with the supernatural among mainline denominations in the 1950s-60s, which spawned the Charismatic movement. Spirit-filled believers migrated not to established Pentecostal churches, but stayed in their own denominations, hoping to vivify them.[144]

Though mysticism runs through the veins of Christian history, there has not been a unanimously held *form* thereof. Models practiced through the centuries have included: hermeneutic; purgative, illuminative, and unitive; Eucharistic; an interior castle with various mansions representing various states of consciousness; a scholastic model of acquired and infused contemplation; the way of beginners, proficients, and perfect; and the charismatically inspired.

CHRISTIAN MYSTICISM AND *THE CLOUD*

How does the mysticism of *The Cloud* compare with other expressions in Church history? *The Cloud* certainly exerts an effort to acknowledge the 'mystery' inherent in Christianity (which will be explicitly explored in chapter four), and to carry on the tradition related to that mystery. Like Gregory of Nyssa (c. 330-395), the church's first real proponent of a systematic mystical theology, the Englishman acknowledges that something of God and His attributes can be known by the mind and sensible means. But because that knowing is only partial, a

---

[144] Newport, *New Age Movement*, 132-133.

state of despair (ανελπιστια)[145] may arise in those who long for deeper intimacy with God; this despair gives rise to the mystical quest. But in both Gregory and *The Cloud* author, this quest is undertaken within a decidedly Christian and Christocentric framework.[146]

Though some of the *modi operandi*[147] advocated by the Englishman in contemplative prayer are foreign to Scripture, such as his club-like usage of sacred words, the author tenaciously clings to the classic propositions of the faith. Doctrinal themes surrounding sin, salvation, forgiveness, repentance, mercy, miracles, holiness, grace, and

> **The Cloud is not intended to be a treatise distinguishing Christianity from non-Christian belief systems, nor one which distinguishes Christian mysticism from non-Christian mysticism.**

many others are regularly referenced. Because *The Cloud* is not intended to be a treatise distinguishing Christianity from non-Christian belief systems, nor one which distinguishes Christian mysticism from non-Christian mysticism, the author writes on the assumption that the encounter with God he promotes is consistent with Christian suppositions. "When you set yourself to this exercise (contemplative prayer), and experience by grace that you are called by God to it, then lift up your heart to God by a humble impulse of love, and *mean* the God who made you and ransomed you, and has in his grace

---

[145] Greek term transliterated *anelpistia*.
[146] Copleston, *History of Philosophy*, 35-36.
[147] Latin: "modes of operation."

called you to this exercise."[148]

Clearly, the Englishman's mysticism is not "the major mystical tradition" of W. T. Stace which holds that in "the introvertive mystical experience the individual self passes beyond itself to become one with the infinite or universal self" (read: monistic pantheism), but "a minority mystical tradition which, while accepting as psychological fact the introvertive experience, insists that therein the individual self is not transcended"[149] (read: theism). Moreover, *The Cloud*'s mysticism is even a subset of the 'minority mystical tradition,' in that it is not only theistic, but Christian. The mysticism of *The Cloud* must be distinguished from that of theistic Islam and Judaism, as it is available only for those who "love Jesus," and believe in "his deity," "his manhood," and "his deity and manhood together";[150] it is available only for those who believe that "all men were lost in Adam, and... are saved and shall be by the power of Christ's passion alone... at the price of his precious blood";[151] it is available only for those who believe that "our Lord ascended bodily into heaven... his body has been raised on high with his soul, without any division."[152]

In spite of his singly Christian orientation, the Englishman does not lend emphasis to or even mention 'the sacramental mystery' which has so characterized much of the Church. Contemplation is an 'inward' experience, an inward work which in and of itself has no external generative or expressive

---

[148] Walsh, *The Cloud*, 133; parentheses and italics mine.
[149] W. T. Stace, *Mysticism and Philosophy* (Philadelphia: Lippincott, 1960), 154-155.
[150] Walsh, *The Cloud*, 125.
[151] Ibid., 116, 171-172.
[152] Ibid., 234-235.

features, though its fruit may be evidenced externally, generating beauty both within and without of contemplatives. They
become attractive, both in appearance and character. People
are honored and delighted to be in their company. They are
also able to discern the character of others as necessary.[153]

In many ways the Englishman reflects the thinking of his
predecessors of the scholastic era, preserving a theological distinction between mysticism and scholasticism. *The Cloud*'s
mode of contemplation certainly influenced the mystic activities of the Quietists. And as the Englishman tends to shy away
from external expressions of ecstasy, he would likely not be a
great supporter of those aspects of contemporary Pentecostalism or Charismaticism, though he would laud their passion for
existential encounters with God.

---

[153] Johnston, *The Cloud*, 117.

CHAPTER FOUR

A PHILOSOPHY OF CHRISTIAN MYSTICISM

A BIBLICAL FRAMEWORK

John Newport suggests biblical thinkers must set themselves to exploring the interaction of rationality and intensive spirituality, "in order to develop a biblical perspective in this area and restudy the meaning of biblical mysticism in relation to its counterfeits."[154] It is to this end that this chapter is devoted.

Most Christians who have dismissed mystic ideas or activities as un-Christian, have done so on the basis of their belief that mysticism is strictly an Eastern monistic or occultic concoction, and/or that it operates outside the bounds of rationality. Thus, they say, mysticism cannot coalesce with or be subject to the rational, propositional truths of the Bible.

While it has already been shown that mysticism has existed in the church since the early fathers, this chapter will demonstrate that the fathers did not instigate the practice or assume it from Neoplatonic, Eastern, or occultic sources, but actually carried on the tradition which is both taught and exemplified in the Bible itself. It will also be demonstrated that

---

[154] Newport, *New Age Movement*, 508.

rational propositions
in the Bible point to a
reality which is supra-
rational (a reality
which will here be re-
ferred to as the 'mysti-

> ... *rational propositions in the Bible point to a reality which is suprarational... and even adjure believers to actively engage that reality.*

cal realm'), *and even adjure believers to actively engage that reality.* The suprarationality suggested here does not equal irrationality, but that which transcends the normative rational capacities of mortal humans, or as Webster puts it: "based on or involving factors not to be comprehended by reason alone."[155]

For contemporary Christians given to existential, mystical aspects of the faith – particularly as expressed in Charismatic or Pentecostal circles – to the neglect of the intellectual, effort will be made to demonstrate that the God they so long to commune with communicates that *engagements with the mystical realm must be both undertaken and assessed in accord with the rational propositions of the Bible.* To deviate from the biblically prescribed path is not only conducive to spiritual deception and idolatry, but is minimally, a flirtation with sheer disobedience to God.

THE MYSTICAL REALM

In seeking to establish the reality of and the biblical propositions demonstrative of the mystical realm, a fresh definition will be offered as to what that realm is: the immaterial,[156] mysterious, invisible, spiritual domain in which God and created

---

[155] "Suprarational," in *Webster's New Collegiate Dictionary*: Springfield, MA: G. & C. Merriam Company, 1977.

[156] 'Immaterial' here must be excepted from its normative, comprehensive

spirits, both good and evil, abide. That the realm is 'mysterious' means not only that mortal humans do not have access to some of its secrets, but that vital elements of the realm transcend the normative rational capacities of mortal humans. In other words, aspects of the realm are suprarational. Even so, this does not mean that elements of the realm cannot be communicated by rational propositions.

Two Kinds of Knowledge, Two Kinds of Wisdom

The Bible speaks of two kinds of knowledge and two kinds of wisdom. In context, these connote two kinds of realms: the earthly realm which is apparent to all humans, and the mystical realm which is predominantly veiled.

The first three chapters of 1 Corinthians bring these facts out in marked relief. In verses 19-25 of chapter one, God discloses through the apostle Paul[157] that 'the world'[158] did not come to know God redemptively through its wisdom. Wise people, scribes, debaters, and all who partake of the wisdom of the world have been made to be as foolish before the wisdom of God. The worldly wisdom of both Jews and Greeks (a biblical metaphor for 'all people') pales before the mysterious,

---

meaning, in that there exists the 'mysterious' phenomenon, per biblical revelation, in which at least one material body does and many more will inhabit this realm. Most specifically, the resurrected Jesus Christ now abides in this domain bodily (though that body is able to bend the laws of physics, as we presently know them), as will all those who have trusted Him unto salvation.

[157] The God-inspired, inerrant nature of the Bible is assumed in the body of this thesis.

[158] 'The world' is a common biblical metaphor for the earthly realm which spurns God and the things of God.

spiritual wisdom of Christ crucified. Christ's work accom-
plished through the cross is considered foolishness by Greeks
and is a stumbling block to Jews. While the historicity of
Christ's crucifixion is well established and was certainly no
mystery to His Jewish or Greek contemporaries, the *meaning*
of His crucifixion was veiled from their sight. And while the
meaning and import of the cross was disclosed through the rationally arranged special revelation of apostolic messengers of
that age and has been handed down to succeeding generations
through the written record of the Bible, there remains a mysterious veil over the eyes of many. Paul goes on to speak of
this veil and of the correspondingly distinct nature of the wisdom which lies behind it in verses 6-8 of chapter two.
Speaking of his procla-
mations of the cross, and
presumably of other
Christian proclamations,
he says that they convey
a wisdom which is "not
of this age, nor of the rulers of this age." Rather,
it is "God's wisdom," "a
mystery" and "hidden";
so much so that "none of

> There exists a dichotomy
> between the natural wis-
> dom of the world which
> is conceptually accessible
> to all, and a mysterious,
> hidden, divine kind of
> redemptive wisdom
> which is reserved for
> those willing to bow
> down to the Lord of all.

the rulers of this age has *understood*."[159] There exists a dichotomy, then, between the natural wisdom of the world
which is conceptually accessible to all, and a mysterious, hidden, divine kind of redemptive wisdom which is reserved for
those willing to bow down to the Lord of all.

---

[159] Italics mine.

This dichotomy is amplified in verses 12-16 of chapter two. Therein Paul distinguishes: 1) the "natural man" from those who have received the Spirit of God; 2) human wisdom from Godly wisdom; and 3) natural knowledge from spiritual knowledge. As a result, "a natural man does not accept the things of the Spirit of God; for they are foolishness to him, and he *cannot understand* (γνῶναι) them, because they are *spiritually discerned.*"[160] While a certain set of data is natural and correspondingly accessible to all humans, another set is beyond the grasp of those who have not been vivified by the Spirit of God. Hence, there are two kinds of knowledge and two kinds of wisdom.

A different twist is lent to this dichotomy in verses 26-31 of chapter one. In His sovereignty and according to His pleasure, God chooses for Himself not many who are wise, mighty, or noble, according to 'the flesh.'[161] Rather, He has chosen and exalts those construed as foolish and weak, per the world's measure, whereby He can demonstrate the lack and shame of those strong things of the world which do not willfully operate under His Lordship. This He does so that any glory conferred might be conferred to Him and not according to the self-elevation of mere creatures. If fellowship with God was attainable through the

> If fellowship with God were attainable through the sheer force of natural intellectual exertion, "the wise" could indeed exult in themselves.

---

[160] Italics and parentheses mine.

[161] 'The flesh' is a metaphor similar to 'the world,' but refers specifically to the people and carnal dispositions of the people who abide in 'the world.'

sheer force of natural intellectual exertion, "the wise" could indeed exult in themselves. But this is not possible. In order "that no man should boast before God," it is "by His doing that you are in Christ Jesus, who became to us wisdom from God, and righteousness and sanctification, and redemption, that, just as it is written, 'Let him who boasts, boast in the Lord.' "

Paul narrows his focus slightly in chapter three. While still speaking of the dichotomy between worldly and spiritual wisdom, in verse 20 the Holy Spirit discloses through Paul that, "The Lord knows the *reasonings* of the wise, that they are useless."[162] So not only is worldly wisdom in general distinct from and inferior to spiritual wisdom, but the rational cognitions (διαλογισμους)[163] of the wise of the world somehow fall short. It appears that reason alone is insufficient to attain those things which endure and pertain to life in Christ. It appears that reason alone cannot breach that hidden, mysterious, spiritual realm in which God abides.

The dichotomous nature of knowledge and wisdom as represented in Scripture is not confined to Pauline texts. Jesus Christ often chose to speak in parables. While parables are but short fictitious stories meant to symbolize or illustrate a point, their point can be less than clear to all hearers by virtue of the symbolism used. And so it was with the parables of Christ – their meaning was a mystery to many. But remarkably, this was Christ's *intent*. When asked by His curious disciples as to why He spoke in a way which obscured meaning from so many, He replied, "To you it has been granted to know the *mysteries* of the kingdom of heaven, but to them it has not been

---

[162] Italics mine.
[163] Greek term transliterated *dialogismous*.

granted."[164]   Luke lends further clarification: Of those who could not understand His mysterious parables, Christ said, "...in order that seeing they may not see, and hearing they may not understand."[165]   Jesus was saying, therefore, that there exist mysteries of another realm to which the masses do not have access; the information of that realm abides out-

> **Jesus was saying that there exist mysteries of another realm to which the masses do not have access.**

side the grasp of normal rational and empirical apprehension.

Two Kinds of Realms

Both Jesus and Paul spoke of a mysterious realm inaccessible to the worldly, but accessible to Christ followers. Paul elucidates this theme by emphasizing the distinction between the mysterious and the natural realms. The inspired apostle declared: "Things which eye has not seen and ear has not heard, and which have not entered the heart of man, all that God has prepared for those who love Him."[166]

While this paraphrase of Isaiahic texts is commonly interpreted as a reference to the glories of heaven, and rightly, what is not so commonly noted is the next verse. Therein Paul states that while the wonders of heaven have historically evaded human perception, such is not so in the new Christian era, "For *to us God revealed them* through the Spirit; for the Spirit searches all things, even the depths of God."[167] The wonders, glories, and mysteries of heaven are now accessible to those

---

[164] Matthew 13:10-11. Italics mine.
[165] Luke 8:10.
[166] 1 Corinthians 2:9.
[167] 1 Corinthians 2:10. Italics mine.

who have believed the gospel, repented, and been reborn! Do any earth-bound Christians now behold these wonders at all times? No. But that question gives rise to 'the mystical task' which is addressed in the next section.

What was once impenetrably veiled from human eyes and ears, has now been made accessible to Christian saints. It is as if the veil between God and humanity has been torn open. It is as if, because it is. All the synoptic gospels record that the veil of the Jewish temple "was torn in two from top to bottom"[168] upon the death of

> **What was once impenetrably veiled from human eyes and ears, has now been made accessible to Christian saints.**

the crucified Jesus. The veil which was torn, not by human hands, literally rent that which separated humans from that most sacred earthly representation of the abode of Yehovah – the Holy of Holies. The curtain was torn to symbolize the access Christians now have to that once forbidden realm, the utterly holy place where God dwells. Christians can now "have confidence to enter the holy place by the blood of Jesus, by a new and living way which He inaugurated for us through the veil."[169]

That mysterious realm constituted a predominant theme of Jesus Christ as He walked the earth. Referred to variously as the kingdom of God or the kingdom of heaven, a core of Christ's mission was to announce the arrival of that domain. The kingdom, He said, was both "at hand," and "in your midst."[170] The coming and work of Jesus, then, served as a

---

[168] Matthew 27:51; Mark 15:38; Luke 23:45.
[169] Hebrews 10:19-20.
[170] Mark 1:15; Matthew 3:2; Luke 17:21; etc.

point of transition in human history. What once was inaccessible and forbidden, was now opened up to those who would accept the gospel. The wonders therein were now available, at least in part, for those who would venture to explore.

Ironically, that the kingdom of God is both "at hand" and "in your midst," adds both mystery and clarity to its nature. That it is at hand connotes

> ...that the kingdom is now in our midst is a less settled phenomenon. If it is here, why can people not see it or touch it?

its futuristic component. Few would debate the Bible's portrayal of a future kingdom to be manifest in the *eschaton*[171] as God comes to literally dwell amongst His chosen people. Such is the most thoroughgoing idea of heaven. But that the kingdom is now in our midst is a less settled phenomenon. If it is here, why can people not see it or touch it? Jesus spoke to this as He answered inquiring Pharisees: "The kingdom of God is not coming with signs to be observed; nor will they say, 'Look, here it is!' or 'There it is!' For behold, the kingdom of God is in your midst."[172] The sense in which the kingdom is now with us is not ascertainable by human empirical percepts. It must be engaged by other means.

The kingdom of God, however, does not comprise the totality of the mystical realm. Satan and his minions are created spirits who have "abandoned their proper abode"[173] by virtue of corrupting themselves through sin. They now dwell in, oversee, and carry out their activities from a portion of the mystical realm the Bible describes in various ways. Satan is

---

[171] Greek: "final scenario in God's plan for the world."
[172] Luke 17:20-21.
[173] Jude 6.

called "the god of this world,"[174] and "the prince of the air";[175] he and his forces rule from "principalities" and "high places."[176] As sin arose in Satan and his cohorts, they were banished from the presence of God. But being immaterial spiritual beings who dwelt in the kingdom of God, God did not banish them into the material, earthly realm. Rather, it appears He created a special domain for them which retains elements of the nature of the mystical realm from which they were cast, but is separate from God and His kingdom. Or as verse 6 of Jude puts it, "And angels who did not keep their own domain, but abandoned their abode, *He has kept in eternal bonds under darkness* for the judgment of the great day."[177] Hence, there exists an expression of the mystical realm which is not the kingdom of God, but is inhabited by darkness and evil.

The Biblical evidence is convincing. There are two realms: one is earthly, common to humanity, and readily accessible both via reason and the senses; the other is the immaterial, invisible, mysterious (at least in part), spiritual domain in which God and created spirits, both good and evil, abide.

THE MYSTICAL TASK

The mystical task is the opportunity afforded to regenerate Christian believers to actively enter into the mystical realm in pursuit of furthering their intimacy with God, enhancing their familiarity with His ways and will, in keeping with His

---

[174] 2 Corinthians 4:4.
[175] Ephesians 2:2.
[176] Ephesians 6:12.
[177] Italics mine.

specially revealed parameters.[178]

It is provocative to note that when the Bible describes God and His activities amongst His people, He is often found veiled in a "cloud."

- God led Israel through the wilderness "in a pillar of cloud by day."[179]
- The Lord said to Moses, "Behold, I shall come to you in a thick cloud."[180]
- "And the glory of the Lord rested on Mount Sinai, and the cloud covered it for six days; and on the seventh day He called to Moses from the midst of the cloud."[181]
- As the ark of the covenant was first placed into the holy place of the temple built by Solomon, accompanied by the worshipful music of the Levites, "the house of Yehovah was filled with a cloud, so that the priests could not stand to minister because of the cloud, for the glory of Yehovah filled the house of God."[182]
- And after Jesus Christ was transfigured before three of His disciples, "a cloud formed and began to overshadow them; and they were afraid as they entered the cloud. And a voice came out of the cloud, saying, 'This is My Son, My Chosen One; listen to Him!' "[183]

These incidents, among others, disclose the hidden, glorious, and awesome status of God. He is not one of whom vision is readily granted. In keeping with *The Cloud* author's suggestions, those who approach Him must be prepared to 'travail

---

[178] 'Specially revealed parameters' is a reference to the operative boundaries disclosed in the Bible.
[179] Exodus 13:21.
[180] Exodus 19:9.
[181] Exodus 24:16.
[182] 2 Chronicles 5:13-14.
[183] Luke 9:34-35.

through the cloud.' This is the mystical task.

In the Old Testament, three primary means of taking on the mystical task are presented: waiting, listening, and worship. Due to spatial constraints, examination of these will be abbreviated.

Waiting: As God, draped in cloud, called Moses to meet Him on the top of Mount Sinai to give him the law, He did so with these words, "Come up to Me on the mountain and remain there, and I will give you the stone tablets..."[184] The Hebrew word for 'remain' in this text, *hayah*, literally means "be." So Moses was instructed to come up before the cloud "and just be," or "just wait." And wait Moses did – for six days! It was not until the seventh day that "He called to Moses from the midst of the cloud."[185] Even with that, Moses was apparently 'in the cloud' for thirty-four days, as he was on the mountain a total of forty! Breaking through the cloud, into the presence of God, often requires patient, purposeful waiting.

Listening: The fiftieth chapter of Isaiah provides a fascinating prophetic glimpse into the *modus operandi*[186] the future Messiah would have in His incarnation:

> The Lord God has given Me the tongue of disciples, that I may know how to sustain the weary one with a word. He awakens Me morning by morning, *He awakens My ear to listen* as a disciple. *The Lord God has opened My ear*; and I was not disobedient, nor did I turn back.[187]

---

[184] Exodus 24:12.
[185] Exodus 24:16.
[186] Latin: "mode of operation."
[187] Isaiah 50:4-5.

Highlighted here is that the efficacy of Christ's earthly ministry would come about, at least in part, due to a particularly acute sensitivity to the 'voice' of God. The emphasis in the pericope is not on the nature of that voice, whether it is audible or not, but on the listening and the hearing. The point is that the Messiah will listen, and be enabled to break into the mystical realm to hear God's voice, and in so doing His ministry will be greatly enhanced.

Worship: The scene recounted above of the dedication of the first temple of Yehovah constructed in Jerusalem conveys a stirring picture of the power of praise and worship. The priests had sanctified themselves; the Levitical singers, clothed in fine linen, joined in unison with trumpets, cymbals, harps, and lyres, making "themselves heard with one voice to praise and to glorify Yehovah."[188]   At this, the cloud came. The house was filled with the Glory. No one could remain standing. The mystical task was well done. The people had reached out to God in worship (human thoughts expressed in song, plus the extra-linguistic medium of music), and He reached down to them with His perceptible, awesome presence.

The reality of a distinction between a rational, mental engagement with God, and a suprarational, spiritual engagement with God is perhaps most clearly made in 1 Corinthians 14. The Corinthian believers had been misusing the χαρισματα,[189] unduly elevating the sensational spiritual gifts, particularly γλωσσαλαλια,[190] to the neglect of the

---

[188]   2 Chronicles 5:13.
[189]   Greek term transliterated *charismata*, and translated as "spiritual gifts."
[190]   Greek term transliterated *glossalalia*, and translated as "speaking in tongues."

'more mundane.' Paul attempts to set the matter in order. First he establishes that speaking in tongues is a genuine and valuable gift; it is a mysterious, spiritual, suprarational language: "For one who speaks in a tongue does not speak to men, but to God; for *no one understands*, but in his spirit *he speaks mysteries.*"[191] And while speaking in tongues has the effect of edifying the speaker,[192] in church gatherings tongues should not be spoken unless an interpretation in the common language is also given. "Otherwise, if you bless in the spirit only, how will the one who fills the place of the ungifted say the 'Amen' at your giving of thanks, since he does not know what you are saying?"[193] Those who pray in a tongue, pray with their spirit, but their mind is unfruitful.[194] Paul concludes:

> What is the outcome then? *I shall pray with the spirit and I shall pray with the mind also; I shall sing with the spirit and I shall sing with the mind also.*[195]

There are two 'mechanisms' by which a Christian can pray, and two mechanisms by which a Christian can sing! Praying or singing with the mind is a clear reference to a rational engagement with the divine, as it can be 'understood' by the ungifted[196] person. They can say "Amen" at the appropriate time. Praying or singing with the spirit is clearly a ref-

---

[191] 1 Corinthians 14:2. Italics mine.
[192] Ibid., v. 4.
[193] Ibid., v. 16.
[194] Ibid., v. 14.
[195] 1 Corinthians 14:15.
[196] 'Ungifted' here refers to those who have not received the spiritual gift of 'interpretation of tongues.'

erence to a suprarational, mysterious engagement with the divine. It is not understood by the rational mind. Thus, the reality of and functional legitimacy of suprarational, mysterious engagements with God are fully supported by the biblical, rational propositions of an inspired apostle. But at the same time, the mind is not to be neglected. It has the very important function of communicating in rational terms that can

> ...the reality of and functional legitimacy of suprarational, mysterious engagements with God are fully supported by the biblical, rational propositions of an inspired apostle.

be understood by all people. Paul simultaneously embraces the suprarational and the rational, the spiritual and the mental. One is not to prevail over the other. Each has its place; each has its role.

Looking again at 1 Corinthians 14:2, Paul not only refers to the synergy of these two capacities, but explicates something of the noetic quality of otherwise suprarational charismatic experiences: "For one who *speaks* in a tongue does not speak to men, but to God; for *no one understands*, but *in his spirit he speaks mysteries*."[197] This mysterious form of speech, incomprehensible to the intellect, nevertheless contains rational data which can be discerned and brought out through translation. Such translation or interpretation is also a spiritual gift.[198] "Therefore let the one who speaks in a tongue pray that he may interpret," because only through such interpretation "may the church receive edifying."[199] Because

---

[197] Italics mine.
[198] 1 Corinthians 14:16.
[199] Ibid., vv. 13, 5.

edification of self and others is a primary goal of the χαρισματα,[200] speaking in rational terms is preferable in an assembly: "In the church I desire to speak five words with my mind, that I may instruct others also, rather than ten thousand words in a tongue."[201]   However, interpreted tongues is equally valuable in an assembly, due also to its ability to edify. The mind and the spirit are to work together in bringing about the goal of edification.

In keeping with the 'mystery' of divine engagement, mystical experiences can be simultaneously noetic and ineffable. Ezekiel's encounters with the spiritual realm often left him nearly speechless, or at least wordless. While as a prophet he was intended to relay what he encountered, the 'otherness' of that data resulted in messages ripe with simile: "like glowing metal"; "like torches darting back and forth"; "like lapis lazuli in appearance"; "like an expanse, like the awesome gleam of crystal,"[202]

> **The mind and the spirit are to work together in bringing about the goal of edification.**

etc. Paul knew of the noetic but ineffable mystic realm first hand. Having been "caught up to the third heaven," or "Paradise," Paul "heard inexpressible words, which a man is not permitted to speak."[203]   So though ineffable on the rational plane, he still encountered information, some form of words or revelation. The result of the mystical task is not meant to be devoid of content.

---

[200] Ibid., vv. 4, 26. Greek: "spiritual gifts."
[201] Ibid., v. 19.
[202] Ezekiel 1:4, 13, 22, 26.
[203] 2 Corinthians 12:2, 4.

BIBLICAL MYSTICISM VERSUS COUNTERFEITS

Christians leery of the mystical task may be so for various reasons. Uninformed lay persons may reject it due to associating 'mysticism' exclusively with the occult. Informed academics or Christian professionals may reject it because of its ethereal, suprarational nature, or because it seems like risky, uncertain terrain upon which to tread. Both objections issue elements of truth. Occult groups and non-Christian religions often do have mystic expressions. And even ordinate Christian mysticism *is* ethereal and suprarational, and contains elements of risk and uncertainty. But these concerns must be tempered in light of Scripture in four main respects.

Firstly, engagements with the mystical realm must be both undertaken and assessed in accordance with the rational propositions of the Bible. This is exemplified in Paul's instruction about the spiritual gift of prophecy. Is this gift to be exercised ad lib? No. It is to be done orderly, in line with the prescription of the apostle: "You can all prophesy *one by one.*"[204] As the mystical realm is entered, and messages received from God, are those messages to be accepted without scrutiny? No. "Let two or three prophets speak, and let the others pass judgment... the spirits of the prophets are subject to the prophets; for God is not a God of confusion."[205] God does not contradict Himself or blur previous revelation. Messages perceived to be mystically received must correspond to that which God has already revealed.[206]

Secondly, the mystical task is not intended to be some

---

[204] 1 Corinthians 14:31.
[205] Ibid., vv. 29, 33.
[206] See Deuteronomy 13:1-5, and Jeremiah 28:1-17.

shady exercise which takes
place only on the fringes of
Christianity. The Bible issues
positive injunctions for believers to take up the mystical task:

> **The Bible issues positive injunctions for believers to take up the mystical task.**

"Earnestly desire the greater gifts"; "I wish that you all spoke in tongues, but even more that you would prophesy"; "I thank God I speak in tongues more than you all"; and "Desire earnestly to prophesy, and do not forbid to speak in tongues."[207]

Thirdly, mystical experiences of leading characters in the early church, and even of Jesus Christ are recorded in the pages of Holy Writ. Subsequent to being led about by the Holy Spirit in the wilderness during a forty day fast, Christ encountered the leader of the evil sphere of the mystical realm. In what could only be considered a supernatural occurrence, the devil "led Him up and showed Him all the kingdoms of the world in a moment of time."[208] The praying Peter "fell into a trance; and he beheld the sky opened up, and a certain object like a great sheet coming down, lowered by four corners to the ground, and there were in it all kinds of four-footed animals..."[209] The term which describes the 'trance' Peter was in is actually the Greek εκστασις,[210] from which the English 'ecstasy' is derived. Thayer defines εκστασις as: "A throwing of the mind out of its normal state; alienation of mind, in which the mind is drawn off all surrounding objects and wholly fixed on things divine."[211]

---

[207] 1 Corinthians 12:31, 14:5, 18, 39.
[208] Luke 4:5.
[209] Acts 10:10ff.
[210] Transliterated *ekstasis*.
[211] Thayer, *Lexicon*, 1614.

The parallel of εκστασις with *The Cloud*'s suggested path to contemplative prayer is obvious. And while the word 'ecstasy' has been variously used and considered in subsequent Christian generations, both positively and negatively, the fact remains that it was the inspired Luke's term of choice in describing the mystical state Peter experienced. The newly converted Paul, likewise, experienced εκστασις while in prayer, in which Christ gave him instructions pertinent to his immediate circumstances.[212] John was "in the Spirit" prior to receiving the wondrous revelations of the apocalypse.[213] Though exactly what John meant by that phrase is difficult to say, it is certain that he was in a state which was not 'natural' or carnal, and which was conducive to interaction with God and His spiritual realm. While mystical

> **While mystical experiences are fantastic, they are not intended to be alien to the lives of Christians who know, love, and walk with a living God.**

experiences are fantastic, they are not intended to be alien to the lives of Christians who know, love, and walk with a living God.

Fourthly, there are Scriptural warnings against *inordinate* mysticism. But every warning is couched in specific terms, namely, that either the *object*, *means*, or *result* of the enterprise was contrary to God's established revelation. Inordinate *objects* of mysticism include any thing which or person who is not Yehovah God. Neither angels, supposed gods, humans, images of gold, animals, nor any created thing are worthy of

---

[212] Acts 22:17-21.
[213] Revelation 1:10.

the worship and spiritual attention reserved for God.[214]
Yehovah said, "You shall have
no other gods before Me."[215] As

> **Yehovah God is to be the sole *object* of mystical pursuit.**

mysticism, in the generic sense, consists of the pursuit of union
or communion with ultimate Reality, to pursue such with that
which is not God is to reckon someone or something other than
Yehovah as ultimate Reality. This is idolatry. Such an offense
may not be isolated to non-Christian religionists. Necro-
mancy, spiritism, and a flirtation with angels have infiltrated
the church in recent years.[216] Efforts directed at communing
or communicating with the dead or angels or any spiritual en-
tity other than God are prohibited: "Do not turn to mediums or
spiritists; do not seek them out to be defiled by them. I am the
Lord your God."[217] Though God may occasionally *send* one
of His angels to communicate with His people,[218] His people
are never to *seek* them out. God is to be the sole *object* of
mystical pursuit.

The *means* by which the only right *object* of mystical pursuit is to be engaged can also be ordinate or inordinate. Along
with those already specified, such as waiting, listening, worship, prayer, and exercising charismatic gifts, biblical means
of mystically encountering God include: imbibing His word,
fasting, meditation, and even enjoying His creative wonders in

---

[214] See Revelation 19:10; Exodus 20:3-6, 23; Daniel 6; and Romans 1:22-25.
[215] Deuteronomy 5:7.
[216] Ron Rhodes, "Close Encounters of the Celestial Kind," *Christian Research Journal* 17 (Spring 1995): 17-23.
[217] Leviticus 19:31.
[218] Genesis 16:9-11; 2 Kings 1:3; Daniel 9:20-23; Luke 1:11-38.

nature.[219] Inordinate mystical means include: consulting or listening to false prophets or teachers, consulting mediums or spiritists, consulting the dead, using drugs, practicing witch-craft, using divination techniques, or self mutilation.[220]

The *results* of mystical enterprises also bear powerfully on their biblical legitimacy. When mystical means are used to acquire spiritual information, that information must corre-spond to that which God has already revealed in the Bible: "When they say to you, 'Consult the mediums and the spiritists who whisper and mutter'... To the law and to the testimony! If they do not speak according to this word, it is because they have no dawn."[221] Focusing on an improper mystical object or using improper mystical means inevitably leads to improper mystical results. The main folly of such results is their turning the mystic or those influenced by the mystic away from Yehovah, i.e., idolatry:

> If a prophet or a dreamer of dreams arises among you and gives you a sign or a wonder, and the sign or the wonder comes true, concerning which he spoke to you, saying, "Let us go after other gods (whom you have not known) and let us serve them," you shall not listen to the words of that prophet or that dreamer of dreams; for Yehovah your God is testing you to find out if you love Yehovah your God with all your heart and with all your soul... But that prophet or dreamer of dreams shall be put to death, because he has counseled rebellion against Yehovah your God... to seduce you from the way in which Yehovah your God commanded you to walk.[222]

---

[219] Acts 4:31; Psalm 119; Matthew 4:1-2; Psalm 4:4, 143:5, etc.
[220] Leviticus 19:31; Deuteronomy 18:9-13; 1 Samuel 28; 1 Kings 18:25-29; Jeremiah 28; Acts 16:16-18; Galatians 5:20, etc.
[221] Isaiah 8:19-20.
[222] Deuteronomy 13:1-5.

Though idolatry is the overarching reason for God's prohibitions against inordinate mysticism, there are also two related reasons: 1) fallen humanity is prone to being deluded by our own imaginings; and 2) it is fully possible to interact with the mystical dimension in the wrong manner, resulting not in contact with God, but with the evil domain of darkness. Concerning reason number one, God forcefully speaks through the Psalmist to those whose imaginings had led them astray: "These things you have done (various evils), and I kept silence; *you thought I was just like you*; I will reprove you, and state the case in order before your eyes. Now consider this, you who forget God, lest I tear you to pieces, and there be none to deliver."[223] It is a grave mistake to allow one's imagination to misperceive or misrepresent the ultimate Reality. As for the second reason, the Bible clearly portrays the possibility of and the heinousness of contacting not God, but spirits of darkness. Such spirits often present themselves as benevolent beings of light and by this the unwary are deceived. The deceitful activities of these malevolent spirits are able to adversely influence even those of a Christian orientation: "The Spirit explicitly says that in the later times some will fall away from

> **It is not only naked idolatry and skewed imaginings which represent inordinate *results* of mysticism, but contact with spiritual forces of darkness and the lies they promulgate.**

the faith, paying attention to deceitful spirits and doctrines of demons."[224] These lying spirits, among other things, strive to

---

[223] Psalm 50:21-22. Italics and parenthesis mine.
[224] 1 Timothy 4:1.

distort truth as represented by sound doctrine. So it is not only naked idolatry and skewed imaginings which represent inordinate *results* of mysticism, but contact with spiritual forces of darkness and the lies they promulgate.

With respect to this last point, religious syncretists are partially correct. There is a 'kernel of metaphysical truth' to be found in the unitive features of mysticism around the world. That truth is that there *is* a suprarational, immaterial, spiritual reality to which unmediated access can be had. Mystical descriptions from diverse religionists which happen to overlap, overlap because they are attempting to describe something of the profundity of reaching a similar reality. The similarity in that reality is that it is the mystical realm; the difference is that the domain of the mystical realm contacted through non-Christian or inordinate mysticism is likely to be not the kingdom of God, but the domain of evil and darkness. But if this is so, how can those who practice unbiblical forms of mysticism report positive experiences? Scripture reveals that the wonder and grandeur of the mystical realm and its inhabitants are so beyond human norms that contact with other created beings of that realm can inspire worship. John the Revelator severally fell at the feet of angels to worship, and was reproved for it.[225] And as Satan, one well acquainted with the majesties of that realm, "disguises himself as an angel of light," and "his servants also disguise themselves as servants of righteousness,"[226] little mystery remains as to how the unwary could be deceived. That such deception occurs illuminates God's motives for forbidding spurious forms of mysticism. It also highlights the

---

[225] Revelation 19:10, 22:9.
[226] 2 Corinthians 11:14-15.

need for biblically prescribed forms of spiritual discernment amongst mystic practitioners, which will be addressed further in the next chapter.

EXISTENTIAL INSIGHTS

In addition to those in Scripture, countless accounts of the personal journeys and revelations of Christian mystics can be plucked from history. While each adds a liveliness to the creeds, this exam must necessarily be confined. It will center on that journey of which I am most expert – my own.

My first recollection of an "unmediated link to the absolute" occurred at a very young age. While walking along a Los Angeles avenue one morning on my way to kindergarten, I pulled my head up and to the right, glancing at an indistinct grayish sky. Something awakened inside of me. "No one," I thought, "No one could know more; no one could know more fully or deeply than me." While a stunning thought for a five year-old, and admittedly having a prideful air to it, I was too young to even entertain the notion of pomposity. The 'knowing more' to which my thoughts referred did not mean some accumulation of naturally acquired data, as my small mind had limited stores of that. Rather, what I sensed, what I knew, had to do with awareness, an awareness of that which really Is, of depth, through and through. I had somehow touched, if even for a moment, that Reality which lies beyond. And insofar as I 'knew' that reality at that moment, however incomplete, no one could know more.

While I was not "in Christ"[227] at that early age, I believe the experience was part of the process by which the Reality was making Himself known to me in a personal way. My subsequent conversion experience was itself of a highly mystical nature.

Having first heard the gospel of the atoning work of Jesus Christ when I was ten years old, I was mightily compelled to positively and immediately respond. At the time, I knew almost nothing of God of a rational, propositional nature; but I still 'knew' it was He who was moving me to respond. But I resisted. Through the exertion of my will, spurred by fear of what other people might think, I resisted God's call. In the aftermath of that dramatic encounter, I remember praying to God that though I knew the gospel to be true (which in retrospect had to be little more than an intuition), I was not yet ready to surrender my life to Him. I had many things I wanted to do. I wanted to live life my way until I was, "Oh, about 24 years old, or so," I told Him.

Not from a Christian or even a religious home, I lived the next fourteen years of my life in typical worldly fashion. One evening, my best friend and I found ourselves in my house after a heavy night of carousing. He lay on one couch, I on another, staring blankly into the flicker of an old black and white television. Then an odd thing happened: starting in the center of my belly, spreading in all directions until it reached my mind, grew this overwhelming wave, this overwhelming compulsion. To do what? To do what I knew I had to do from the first time I heard the gospel – publicly surrender my life to the

---

[227] A favorite phrase of the apostle Paul, describing what he understands to be the spiritual status of all the elect. See Romans 6:11; 1 Corinthians 1:30; Galatians 3:28; Ephesians 2:10, etc.

Lord and Savior of humankind. After a series of unsuccessful starts at accommodating that wave, triumph occurred as I stated out loud, "Jesus is my Savior." Immediately I was aware of being filled, of being washed on the inside, from head to toe with clean, warm Light, even Life itself. I felt as if ten thousand bricks had been flung from my chest. In saying those words, I did not jump in; the Lord came and grabbed me, engulfed me in His love and took me as His own. I knew I was safe – forever. I was 24 years old.

It was not until after my conversion that the rational propositions of the Christian faith, particularly as rendered by the Bible, became prominent in my thinking. Hence,

> He who had enlivened my spirit by His Spirit was now renewing my mind in accord with His mind. I came to see that the Christian faith was not only alive, but that it made sense.

though fully unintentional, my experience with God and His realm assumed an Anselmian form: *credo ut intelligam*.[228] Whereas the Bible had once been a book I rarely read, due to its convicting me that I was not right with God, post-conversion it became an irreplaceable and unequaled source of knowledge, wisdom, and truth. He who had enlivened my spirit by His Spirit was now renewing my mind in accord with His mind. I came to see that the Christian faith was not only alive, but that it made sense. Christianity is not only existentially viable, but rationally consistent and empirically verifiable.[229]

---

[228] Latin: "I believe in order to understand."

[229] This tri-fold verificational nature of Christianity is forwarded by

As my Christian walk commenced in earnest, my personal interaction with the Most High was varied, both in form and depth. There came a point, however, when I reached an impasse. In my deepest moments of communion with God, a road block began to make itself known. I could get so far, I could get so close, and no further. The impediment? Words. Language. My words and my language have limited capacities, as do those of all humans. We can go so far in communicating with another, beyond which words must be left behind. Given this, our species has developed and utilized other means, such as music, painting, dancing, and even sex, to express those things that words alone cannot.

If complete bilateral understanding amongst human beings is impossible through verbalization alone, do not similar impediments exist in our relationships with God? True, in the God-man relationship, the impediment is monodirectional, as God does not have communicative limits; it nevertheless exists on the human end of the process. Whether we speak or listen, the depth of human linguistic interaction goes only as far as our respective linguistic capacities.

> **Whether we speak or listen, the depth of human linguistic interaction goes only as far as our respective linguistic capacities.**

Thus, I found myself wanting to get more intimate with God than my language would allow. In my disdain for this

---

Edward John Carnell, Gordon Lewis and others. See: Gordon R. Lewis, *Testing Christianity's Truth Claims* (New York: University Press of America, 1976), 176-284.

linguistic limitation, I determined, in my praying, to lay language aside. It was not easy, because it was not natural. But in my hunger for intimacy I pressed on. I did not know what would happen or how it would happen, but I was determined to pursue whatever means to that glorious end – as long as those means were not outside the parameters laid down by that End, in His word, the Bible. The result? I broke through.   Or as

> **God is aware of our linguistic limits. In His desire to facilitate a depth of intimacy we could not naturally have, He allows His Spirit to intercede for us in a supralinguistic way.**

Scripture puts it, "In the same way the Spirit also helps our weakness; for we do not know how to pray as we should, but the Spirit Himself intercedes for us with groanings too deep for words; and He who searches the hearts knows what the mind of the Spirit is, because He intercedes for the saints according to the will of God."[230]   God is aware of our linguistic limits. In His desire to facilitate a depth of intimacy we could not naturally have, He allows His Spirit to intercede for us in a supralinguistic way.

Like *The Cloud* author, part of the challenge I faced in breaking through to God was the constant onslaught of distracting thoughts. But as I determined to lay language aside, so I knew I needed to lay distracting thoughts aside. But rather than the techniques suggested by the Englishman of batting them out of the way with the monosyllabic 'clubs' of 'God' or 'sin,' I did so through the use of imagery. Believing I was led by the Spirit in this technique, I came to imagine, as gently as

---

[230] Romans 8:26-27.

possible, a still pond. And upon this pond lay an open flower. The flower was representative of me – open to heaven, still, calm. And as I, the flower, lay there open before heaven, I did not know what was to follow. But as I quietly waited, I was astounded to perceive the clouds opening up, and shafts of light began to ever so elegantly pour down upon me. And so commenced a supralinguistic, suprarational, intimate interaction with He whom I so sought.

EVALUATION OF THE EXISTENTIAL ELEMENT

Concerning mystical events, the studies of William James reaffirm the power of what I and so many others have experienced: "They are as convincing to those who have them as any direct sensible experiences can be, and they are, as a rule, much more convincing than results established by mere logic ever are."[231] Though not all have them, those who do regard them "as genuine perceptions of truth, as revelations of a kind of reality which no adverse arguments, however unanswerable by you in words, can expel from your belief."[232] This is apparently true even of the drug induced variety advanced by Braden. Whether hallucinogens actually open a portal to the mystical realm of spirits (which is entirely possible, particularly given the biblical prohibitions against φαρμακεια[233] – the use of drugs for spiritual practices)[234] or just simulate such, the impact seems the same.

---

[231] James, *Religious Experience*, 72.
[232] Ibid.
[233] A Greek term transliterated *pharmakeia*.
[234] Galatians 5:20; Revelation 18:23.

But again, while the effect on humans entering the mystical/spiritual realm may be universally powerful, it does not diminish the reality that there are two domains within that realm which may be engaged – one evil, and one godly – and that the Bible prohibits engaging the evil domain by prohibiting ungodly objects, means, or results of mysticism. Further, a remarkable thing about Christianity, in contraposition to James' assertion, is that rationality need not be left at the door regarding mystical enterprises. While unanswerable arguments may be forwarded against inordinate mysticism (Christian or non-Christian), that form of mysticism which corresponds with a biblical object, means, and result *corresponds* with extra-mystical data, whether rational or empirical (even though there remains, by its very nature, a suprarational element to mystical experiences).

The inordinate form of mysticism which purports a pantheistic, monistic, undifferentiated Reality with which the mystic metaphysically merges, simply cannot be supported by lan-

> **The inordinate form of mysticism which purports a pantheistic, monistic, undifferentiated Reality... simply cannot be supported by language, logic, or empirical evidence.**

guage, logic, or empirical evidence. The moment such mystics speak in an effort to support their case, they at once disconfirm their case, as the act of speaking necessarily infers differentiation. Speaking or any form of communication entails the attempt to convey information from one agent to *another* agent. To be logically consistent, such mystics' only recourse would be to silently melt into the carpet upon which they stand, in effect, becoming part of the incommunicable and impersonal

That. But as such a 'melting' is impossible, monistic mysticism also fails the empirical test.

Ordinate Christian mysticism, on the other hand, corresponds with extra-mystical, rational and empirical data. Because ordinate Christian mysticism acknowledges an all-powerful yet personal God who is metaphysically distinct from His creation, and who created human beings in His image as distinct persons, communicating one's mystical experiences (at least those elements which are not ineffable) to others does not of necessity disconfirm those experiences. As a differentiated agent, it is logically consistent to have unique, subjective experiences and to speak about them. And because such differentiation corresponds with observable sensory data – at last count, there were over seven billion individual human beings in the world, not a homogenous One – it passes the empirical test as well.

A CONCERT OF REASON AND MYSTICISM

To ask: Is mystical experience to prevail over reason? or, Is reason to prevail over mystical experience? is to ask the wrong questions. From the evidence at hand, it appears that both faculties are fundamental to the human condition, ordained by God,

> **God has given us minds and expects us to use them. God has given us spiritual capacities and expects us to use them.**

and ordered by God to work together. God has given us minds and expects us to use them. God has given us spiritual capacities and expects us to use them. The question, then, is not which should prevail over the other, but how is the concert of reason and mysticism to be conducted?

A concert, by nature, does not entail one instrument prevailing over another, but one instrument complimenting the others. Though the violinist may take pride in her 'prevalence' over the oboist, because she plays a more apparent and quantitatively greater role, such is only exemplary of a shortsighted egoism, as the rich tones offered by the oboe serve as no other instrument can to *enhance* the melodies of the violin. It is only as each works in concert that the whole performance becomes more beautiful. But if such complimentary roles are abandoned for the sake of contest, the work as a whole is thwarted, and the potential of both instruments diminished.

So just as the rational propositions of the Bible drive us to acknowledge the existence of a mystical realm and to pursue the mystical task, they must also be used to direct us to the only proper *object* of that pursuit, to

> **Christian mysticism begins and ends with Bible-based rational activity.**

use the proper *means* in that pursuit, and to scrutinize any revelation, imperatives, or experiences *resulting* from that pursuit. Christian mysticism begins and ends with Bible-based rational activity.

As C. A. Beckwith insightfully comments, "All religion depends on revelation of some sort, real or assumed... When, however, religion depends only on historicity and tradition, it becomes barren, legalistic, and lifeless. It accordingly needs a third element if it is to become a living thing to the individual. This is found in personal, inward experience, which is itself a secondary form of revelation."[235] **Ordinate mystical experience serves as the free-flowing life-blood of Christianity which is then properly contained and distributed to the body through the established and well-ordered arteries of reason.**

---

[235] Beckwith, *Schaff-Herzog*, "Mysticism."

CHAPTER FIVE

THE CLOUD IN RETROSPECT

Thus far, the role of reason in *The Cloud of Unknowing* has been explored by looking both into *The Cloud* and into mystical expressions surrounding that work. We will now revisit our point of departure with a, hopefully, fresh and properly ordered perspective on the interplay of reason and mysticism, for the purposes of considering how this particular piece of fourteenth century literature may either contribute to or depart from that perspective.

THE CLOUD'S CONTRIBUTIONS

THE CRUX OF *THE CLOUD*

The Cloud is often misrepresented by commentators and critics, by focusing excessively on its apophatic theology. Though the *via negativa* comprises a portion of the author's doctrine, to center on that misses his point. His point, his aim, is encounter with God Himself. And apophaticism, he believes, is simply part of the means by which God can best be encountered.

The Englishman would have his students know that with or without negation, God Himself is more precious than

thoughts of God.[236] Consider a typical human romance. Infatuation with a member of the opposite sex often includes rev-
eling in and becoming excited
by thoughts of that person, perhaps to the degree that entertain-
ing oneself with those thoughts
becomes more precious than the
person who is being thought of.
Such misappropriate forms of

> **God must never
> take second-place to
> anything, even to
> thoughts of Him,
> however exalted
> they may be.**

infatuation must never do with God. God must never take sec-
ond-place to anything, even to thoughts of Him, however exalted they may be. It must never be forgotten that thoughts of
God are not God; so to satisfy ourselves with mere thoughts
seems a form of disrespect to and underappreciation of God; it
seems less than the premium expression of love.

Though many contemporary evangelicals may object to
the Englishman's lauding of contemplative prayer and the
preeminent place he gives it in the scheme of things, such objections are open to question. If consideration is given to the
ultimate authority, Jesus Christ, He made it clear that the
preeminent purpose of humans is to love God.[237] Just as Christ
chastened the hardworking Ephesian church for "leaving their
first love,"[238] wise contemporary Christians might ask if their
love for God has been displaced by good works like evange-
lism, church growth, addressing social concerns, preaching,
political activism, and family development. While all these,

---

[236] Johnston, *The Cloud*, 61.
[237] Matthew 22:36-40.
[238] Revelation 2:4.

as the Englishman would say, are worthy activities, in themselves they fall short of God's highest call; they fall short of
reaching after God Himself; they fall short of communing with
the Most High. Mary did indeed choose the best part.

In the Lukan account of Jesus coming to dine with Mary
and Martha,[239] Martha was busying herself with good works,
making all the physical preparations for serving her esteemed
guest. Mary, in contrast, found herself enrapt with the Master
Himself, and could not pull herself away from nestling at His
feet. While the indignant Martha implored the Lord to scold
her sister, Jesus set
the matter in order.
It was Martha who
needed the scolding,
albeit, a gentle one.
Though there are a
great many things a
person could do with

> **Though there are many *im-
> portant* things a person can
> do in this life, there is only
> one *necessary* thing – sitting
> at the Master's feet, loving,
> listening to, and nurturing
> one's relationship with Him.**

Jesus Christ coming over for dinner, Mary had chosen the
most important. "Martha, Martha," Jesus said, "you are wor-
ried and bothered by so many things; but only a few things are
necessary, really only one, for Mary has chosen the good part,
which shall not be taken away from her."[240] Though there are
many *important* things a person can do in this life, there is only
one *necessary* thing – sitting at the Master's feet, loving, listening to, and nurturing one's relationship with Him.

It also appears true, as *The Cloud* author purports, that

---

[239] Luke 10:38-42.
[240] Luke 10:41-42.

worthy works are born out of genuine love of God.[241] However, if we reverse this order the results are often incommensurate. As one faithfully attends to contemplative work, the author is certain that "you will know when to begin and end every other activity."[242] Good 'active' works will pour out of good contemplation, but not vice-versa. Christ appears to demonstrate this by giving the impression that He was on an unseen timetable, doing everything in perfect accord with the Father.[243] Jesus' perfect 'doing' was preceded by His 'being' with the Father for regular and lengthy intervals.[244]

So the Englishman is not without recognition of the value of extra-contemplative activities. "Not that he should ever abandon contemplation entirely – for this could not be done without great sin – but sometimes charity will demand that he descend from the heights of this work

> As a proper love for humanity grows out of spending time with God, allotting portions of our time toward the welfare of others will naturally follow.

to do something for his fellow man."[245] We are not to balance contemplation with love of humanity, as that would be sinful, a *disordo amoris*.[246] God is to be loved preeminently, and neighbors secondarily.[247] But as a proper love for humanity grows out of spending time with God, allotting portions of our

---

[241] Johnston, *The Cloud*, 64.
[242] Ibid., 101.
[243] See John 2:4, 4:32-34, 5:19-20, 6:38, 8:28-29.
[244] Mark 1:35, 6:32, 46, 9:2-8, 14:32-42; Luke 4:1-14, 6:12.
[245] Johnston, *The Cloud*, 81.
[246] Latin for "disordered love."
[247] See Matthew 22:36-40; Mark 3:31-35; and Luke 14:26.

time toward the welfare of others will naturally follow.

The mysticism of *The Cloud* is dramatically distinct from the monistic, "major mysticism" of Stace on this count. Whereas love for humanity and corresponding good works naturally follow from *The Cloud*'s Christian mysticism (Stace's "minority mystical tradition"), such cannot be for the consistent monistic mystic. For the consistent monist, time, history, words, other humans, and even their own lives must be irrelevant illusions (the Hinduistic *maya*),[248] as all is One. As such, the mysticism of monists provides no basis upon which to reach out lovingly to others. Monists cannot be charged with *disordo amoris*, as for them there is no *amoris*!

Disordo amoris, however, is expressed in contemporary Western culture, and has to a formidable degree been adopted by church constituents in regard to romantic love. Romantic love is popularly portrayed as the great goal of life: "If you find your soul-mate or lust-mate, that is all you will ever need." Provocatively, such notions were apparent in the Englishman's day as well. Part of his thrust in placing creatures below 'the cloud of forgetting' while approaching God is made in response to this erroneous propensity. In something of an explanation of the genesis of and results of original sin, the Englishman says that,

> Before he sinned, man was master and lord of all creatures but he yielded to the evil suggestion of these creatures and disobeyed God. And now when he wishes to obey God he feels the drag of created things. Like arrogant pests they annoy him as he reaches out for God.[249]

---

[248] Winfried Corduan, *Neighboring Faiths* (Downers Grove, IL: InterVarsity Press, 1998), 198.

[249] Johnston, *The Cloud*, 85.

Pleasurable thoughts of other humans can pose a danger if those thoughts are mistaken as "all you could ever want."[250]

A CONCERT IN *THE CLOUD*?

How does *The Cloud* author express or fail to express "the concert of reason and Christian mysticism"?

The Englishman acknowledges that contemplation can be a dangerous arena for the novice. An evil domain exists and may be unwittingly engaged. If novice contemplatives misunderstand the interior life, and try too hard to see and hear interior things, they may open themselves up to the evil one and his deceptions. Deceptions may take the form of pseudo-experiences and false knowledge, and may arise not only through excessive effort, but by pride, sensuality, or intellectual conceit.[251] Fantastic lights or sounds, odors or tastes may be perceived. "For the devil may excite his passions and arouse all sorts of bizarre sensations in his breast or bowels, his back, loins, and other organs."[252] Such a person becomes "so satiated with lies that vain thoughts do not really trouble him."[253] In essence, the Englishman sees such folk as sincere, but sincerely deceived.

Deception can also arise if initiates apply their imaginations to excess. Imagination depicts the likeness of things. These images are contained in the Mind.

> Before original sin, Imagination cooperated completely with Reason... it faithfully reflected each image as it really

---

[250] Ibid., 62-63.
[251] Ibid., 105-106.
[252] Ibid., 115.
[253] Ibid.

was and thus Reason was never deceived in its judgments by the distorted likeness of any material or spiritual thing. Now, however, this integrity of our nature is lost.[254]

Imagination now distorts images of material things, and it also creates counterfeits of spiritual things, or even conjures up sheer fantasies. Apart from grace the Imagination is subject to great error. Thus, the Imagination of contemplative neophytes may be unruly, drawing them away to deceitful thoughts and images, imagining heavenly scenes, or the appearance of God or of angels. But as neophytes are trained by the discipline of contemplation, meditating faithfully "on their own human frailty, the Passion of Christ, his transcendent goodness, and the other truths of the interior life, Reason is gradually healed, regaining its rightful ascendancy over the Imagination."[255]

Thus, *The Cloud* author admits that while the weakness of human contemplatives leaves them susceptible to error – whether being deceived by dark forces of the mystical realm or by their own imagination – those weaknesses can be countered by meditating upon the rational and fundamental propositions of the Christian faith, just as suggested by 'the concert.'

The Englishman also issues warnings about the results of contemplation, particularly as manifest in behaviors. Pseudo-contemplatives most often exhibit eccentric behavior, whereas God's true friends carry on with simple grace. Such eccentricity may include: frightful looks upon the face, blank stares, heads drooping to one side, making shrill sounds, whining or

---

[254] Ibid., 132.
[255] Ibid.

whimpering, or effeminate gestures.[256] This indictment of 'eccentric behavior,' while consistent with the Englishman's advocacy of a gentle, interior communion with God, does not necessarily correspond with multiple accounts of biblical characters who had 'an unmediated encounter with God.' Many exhibited extreme behaviors. The prophet Isaiah went about barefoot and naked for three years, in keeping with instruction he received from Yehovah.[257] God directed Ezekiel to lie on his side for immense periods of time, as in 390 days on his left side and 40 days on his right, as physical acts signifying spiritual functions.[258] A New Testament prophet, Agabus, bound his own hands and feet together with the belt of Paul, per the Holy Spirit, seeking to portray Paul's fate if he carried out his plans to go to Jerusalem.[259] The presence or absence of extreme behaviors, then, is not in and of itself indicative of an ordinate encounter with Yehovah.

The Cloud author does not promote the pursuit of mystical visions or other extravagant spiritual manifestations. If contemplatives were sufficiently astute, exceptional manifestations would not be necessary, as the deep spiritual meanings signified by visions would be ascertainable in other ways (though he does not specify what those other ways might be). Even so, we are not to despise genuine "spiritual fruit."[260] On this, the Englishman is also on the conservative side of the charismatic scale (something mystics are rarely accused of), in that the New Testament actually instructs Christians to *pursue*

---

[256] Ibid., 116.
[257] Isaiah 20:2-4.
[258] Ezekiel 4:4-6.
[259] Acts 21:10-11.
[260] Johnston, *The Cloud*, 123-124.

the χαρισματα,[261] including the 'sensational' ones.[262]

Included in the applicable advice to today's Christian mystics advanced by *The Cloud* author is: Consolation of the senses or even of the spirit during contemplation should be enjoyed, but never relied upon, lest too much stock be taken in those consolations or they come to be expected too frequently.

> To seek *experiences* rather than God is as much a sin as seeking *thoughts* rather than God. Hence, excesses on both the mystical and intellectual sides are to be avoided.

If this occurs, it is possible that what Christian mystics end up seeking is the experience rather than God.[263] To seek *experiences* rather than God is as much a sin as seeking *thoughts* rather than God. Hence, excesses on both the mystical and intellectual sides are to be avoided.

The synergy of mysticism and reason is somewhat slighted, however, as the Englishman considers what it is that protects contemplatives from evil forces during their work. How is it that contemplatives can be certain that external forces cannot hurt them?

> ...because the source of authentic consolation is the reverent, loving desire that abides in a pure heart. This is the work of Almighty God wrought without recourse to techniques and therefore it is free of the fantasy and error liable to befall a man in this life.[264]

---

[261] Greek: "spiritual gifts."
[262] See I Corinthians 12:31, 14:1, 39.
[263] Johnston, *The Cloud*, 112.
[264] Ibid., 110.

Furthermore, as the contemplative is occupied "in the blind, reverent, joyful longing of contemplative love... this love itself will enable you to discern unerringly between good and evil."[265] Perceptions from uncertain sources will either be approved or disapproved "from within by the Holy Spirit."[266] By virtue of the fact that contemplatives pursue God blindly, reverently, joyfully, and lovingly, they can rest assured that the Holy Spirit will give them the supernatural ability to discern the source of perceptions they may have. But is this so?

The reality of the spiritual faculty of 'discernment of spirits' is revealed in Scripture. The Holy Spirit supernaturally endows some believers with the acute ability to determine the nature or orientation of spirits in question – but only *some* believers: "For *to one* is given the word of wisdom through the Spirit... and *to another* the distinguishing of spirits."[267] This being so, how are the ungifted to discern good from evil spirits? The Englishman, at least in the passage in question, offers no answer; the Bible, however, does. While only some have the supernatural, spiritual gift, God makes provision for all His people to discern spirits, and that provision is markedly propositional and rational: "By this you know the Spirit of God: every spirit that confesses that Jesus Christ has come in the flesh is from God; and every spirit that does not confess Jesus is not from God."[268]

The mystic gifted with the supernatural ability to discern spirits, then, can rely upon the power and enabling of the Holy

---

[265] Ibid.
[266] Ibid., 110-111.
[267] 1 Corinthians 12:8-10.
[268] 1 John 4:2-3.

Spirit to determine the source of spirits or percepts encountered in the mystical task. But the wise mystic adds yet another armament to his arsenal – the rational propositions of the word of God.[269]

The Englishman should not be reproved too quickly or harshly for this oversight, however, as he displays an orthodoxy that would put many current evangelicals to shame, whether speaking of the divine-human relationship or tenets of the faith. His phraseology, penned

> **The Englishman should not be reproved too quickly or harshly... as he displays an orthodoxy that would put many current evangelicals to shame.**

some 650 years ago, even rings evangelical: "Basically, love means a radical personal commitment to God. This implies that your will is harmoniously attuned to his in an abiding contentedness and enthusiasm for all he does."[270] And he consistently points to orthodox doctrine: Christ's full humanity and deity, His glorified humanity and current position in heaven, His bodily resurrection, the immortal nature of His resurrected body, and that believers shall experience the same.[271]

And reflecting the Roman view of authority in the Church common to his day, the Englishman stresses the importance of not being too independent – of not relying too heavily upon one's own learning. The edicts of the Church and her leader-

---

[269] 'Wise' in this case should not be construed as applying only to the intellectually inclined, but to all Christians who abide by the counsel of God's word.

[270] Johnston, *The Cloud*, 111.

[271] Ibid., 124-125.

ship must be listened to, lest the seeker fall into deception.[272] While Protestant evangelicals would take exception to the source of authority specified, the fact that the Englishman recognizes the need for an authority external to oneself while engaging in spiritual endeavors is supportive of the 'concert' motif.

DANGERS IN *THE CLOUD*

THE NATURE OF 'UNION' WITH GOD

Some of history's most notable Christian mystics have been demeaned, and properly, for going too far with *unio mystica*.[273] Meister Eckhart, for example, developed a doctrine which bordered on synthesis between the soul and God. Consequently, his thinking is often compared to monistic Hindu and Buddhist mystics.[274]

How fares the Englishman in this respect? A notable feature of *The Cloud* is the author's lack of concern for specifying the metaphysical implications of his teachings. This may in part be due to his Christian assumptions and those he presupposes of his Christian students. If the Englishman believes he knows the metaphysical relationship between God and Christians, he seemingly assumes his students know as well. After all, *The Cloud* is not a theological or philosophical treatise, but an instruction manual about how best to commune with God.

Nevertheless, with a little digging, a fair picture of the metaphysical implications of contemplative prayer can be

---

[272] Ibid., 120-121.
[273] Latin for "mystical union."
[274] Newport, *New Age Movement*, 123-124.

found. The first textual reference which bears on this issue is right on the surface, spelled-out in the original title: "A Book of Contemplation called The Cloud of Unknowing which is about that cloud within which one is united to God."[275] Though wary evangelicals may bristle at the term 'united' when used in this way, several responses would be in order. First, it is unclear as to what way the author is using 'united' in the immediate context. Second, there is in fact a unity between the believer and God which is positively referenced in the Bible. Jesus prayed for a union between believers and God: "That they may all be one; even as Thou Father, art in Me, and I in Thee, that they also may be in Us... I in them, and Thou in Me, that they may be perfected in unity."[276] In short, not all references to a unity of believers with God can be counted as heretical. But if this is so, what kind of a unity was being advocated by Christ? A monistic union must be immediately dismissed. Christ was speaking to His Father of their presently existing union: "... as Thou Father, *art* in Me." Speaking to another distinct person cannot occur short of individuation. And as Christ and the Father were/are individuated while at once being united, necessitates that that union be something other than a meta-physical melding of persons.

> It is a non-metaphysical, relational unity with the Godhead that Christ was praying His followers might also experience.

It must, per the context, be a *relational* unity. Hence, it is a non-metaphysical, relational unity with the Godhead that Christ was praying His followers

---

[275] Johnston, *The Cloud*, 33.
[276] John 17:21, 23.

might also experience.

The Cloud author, however, is represented by commentator James Walsh as falling into the synthesis trap: "There is to be no room left for any separate consciousness of ourselves... The contemplative does not 'see God'; he enters into God's seeing."[277] Self disappears as subject and is known, if at all, only as object. But the Englishman, Walsh says, is not concerned with the ramifications of this synthesis: "It is God's business, not ours, to safeguard our distinctness from himself... But this 'self-naughting,' though it means that we must lose our consciousness of ourselves, is actually the way that we 'become' ourselves."[278] Walsh's interpretation of the Englishman, though, is eisegetical and not born out by *The Cloud* itself, as will be shown below.

The Englishman does advocate a form of 'self-forgetting,' but not the form Walsh suggests. Part of *The Cloud*'s prescription in the contemplative pursuit of God is, as has already been specified, placing all creatures and thoughts of creatures below oneself in a 'cloud of forgetting.' Only as this is done can God be pursued with a 'naked intent,' devoid of distractions. As humans, including seekers themselves, are but creatures, self must also be placed under this cloud. But this is not easy. Because of its natural presence in consciousness, self is usually the last to go. Thus, self-forgetting can occur in the seeker only through God's grace as it is expressed in a "strong, deep, interior sorrow... *that he is*."[279]

Seekers should have a sorrow over being because it is one's being which most consistently prevents a true

---

[277] Walsh, *The Cloud*, xxii.
[278] Ibid.
[279] Johnston, *The Cloud*, 104.

knowledge and feeling of God. Seekers constantly find their knowing and feeling occupied with themselves, and self is "a foul, stinking lump... which must always be hated and despised and forsaken."[280] Thus, the contemplative "feels the burden of himself so tragically that he no longer cares about himself if only he can love God."[281] It is in and because of such sorrow over being that the contemplative can come to his proper place of selflessness.

Yet, the Englishman makes it clear that seekers are never to desire not to be, "for this is the devil's madness and blasphemy against God."[282] Seekers are to rejoice that they are, with a grateful heart, for the goodness and gift of existence. Paradoxically, the Englishman adds, "At the same time, however, he desires unceasingly to be freed from the knowing and feeling of his being."[283]

Though, as stated, Walsh's monistic interpretation of *The Cloud* seems extreme, there are several troubling items in the Englishman's doctrine which deserve unpacking. That the author believes there is an advantage to being sorrowful in realizing that 'one is,' is very disturbing. To regret one's existence is to regret God's won-

> We *are* only because God made us *to be*, and to be sorrowful over that, far from a benefit, is more akin to a sin.

derful gift of life. We *are* only because God made us *to be*, and to be sorrowful over that, far from a benefit, is more akin

---

[280] Ibid.
[281] Ibid.
[282] Ibid.
[283] Ibid.

to a sin. But with this acknowledged, it must also be acknowledged that the Englishman concedes that seekers *are never* to
desire not to be, as such desires are blasphemous and devilish.
But are not his positions antithetical? Can it be sinful to desire
not to be, while advantageous to be sorrowful over being? A
resolution to this paradox will be offered, but only as a contingent resolution, in that *The Cloud* author does not supply sufficient information on his respective positions to render a de-
finitive response. Some inference and conjecture must be utilized.

The paradox can be resolved if two aspects of humanness
are granted to inhere in the Englishman's teachings: 1) the natural, sinful nature, and 2) the spiritual, regenerate, godly nature. His reference to self being "a foul, stinking lump which
must be hated, despised, and forsaken," surely qualifies as a
reference to aspect number one. To imagine, then, that such a
cogent author would in the same breath and on the same page
insist that seekers are never to desire not to be, if 'being' only
consists of that which is to be hated, despised, and forsaken,
simply does not follow. And though he never inserts the dual
nature hypothesis in this section for clarification, that hypothesis could reasonably be assumed for the Englishman because
a primary source of his, the Bible, clearly teaches the same –
a dual human nature in which the worldly and sinful aspect is
to be hated, despised, and forsaken, while the regenerate, spiritual, and godly aspect is to be gratefully embraced.[284] Coin-
cidingly, it is "the knowing and feeling" of the sinful self from
which believers are to seek freedom. Walsh's faulty portrayal
of the Englishman promoting a dissolution of self into God

---

[284] Romans 7:14-25; Ephesians 2:1-10, 4:17-32; Colossians 3:1-17.

likely arises from an insufficient recognition of Christianity's theology of a dual human nature amongst the regenerate, and a failure to recognize the self-contradiction which results within *The Cloud* if such a duality doctrine is not incorporated.

The juncture at which *The Cloud* presents its most explicit metaphysical stance on *unio mystica*,[285] concerns the 'high point' of contemplation, in which there is 'contact' with God. In speaking of this high point, the Englishman asserts that seekers become "almost divine."[286] It is through contemplation-born grace that one acquires that which is impossible by nature – "union with God in spirit, in love, and in oneness of desire."[287]

> You may in a sense truly be called divine. The Scriptures, in fact, do say this.[288] Yet, of course, you are not divine in the same way God himself is; he without origin or end as defined by nature. You, however, were brought into being from nothingness at a certain moment in time. Moreover, after God had created you with the Almighty power of his love, you make yourself less than nothing through sin. Because of sin you have not deserved anything, the all-merciful God lovingly re-created you in grace, making you, as it were, divine and one with him for time and eternity. Yet, though you are truly one with him through grace, you remain less than him by nature.[289]

Though the author certainly refers to unitive features resulting

---

[285] Latin for "mystical union."

[286] Johnston, *The Cloud*, 135.

[287] Ibid.

[288] Though the Englishman cites no references, it is assumed he was referring to Psalm 82:6; John 10:31-36; and 2 Peter 1:4.

[289] Johnston, *The Cloud*, 135.

from the contemplative process, he is careful to retain onto-
logical distinctions between believers and God. Believers become 'almost divine,' and divine 'in a sense,' but are not divine in the same way God is. God is divine by nature. He is
creator, we are created; He is eternal, we once were not. Whatever stature believers have, it is solely by God's grace.
Though believers are made one with Him in spirit, love, and
desire, they remain less than God by nature.

Hence, Walsh's monistic interpretation of *The Cloud* fails
again, per *The Cloud*'s own statements about *unio mystica*. By
this interpreter's measure, the Englishman remains on orthodox soil.

PROBLEMS WITH THOUGHTLESSNESS

There are two aspects of 'thoughtlessness' which are ap-
ropos to *The Cloud* and which will be addressed in this section:
1) thoughtlessness as a *means* of contemplative prayer, and 2)
thoughtlessness regarding the *result* of contemplative prayer.
Point number one first:

> Your part is to be as wood to a carpenter or a home to a
> dweller. Remain blind during this time, cutting away all
> desire to know, for knowledge is a hindrance here. Be con-
> tent to feel this mysterious grace sweetly awaken in the
> depths of your spirit. Forget everything but God and fix on
> him your naked desire, your longing stripped of all self-in-
> terest.[290]

The Englishman advocates a position many evangelical thinkers would deem dangerous – a thoughtless, proposition-less

---

[290] Ibid., 92.

state, in which the seeker opens him/herself up to spiritual forces. *Cloud* proponents might immediately counter that the otherwise dangerous state of cognitive emptiness is remedied by the phrase "forget everything *but God*," and such proponents would be partially correct. There is a caveat to thoughtlessness in the Englishman's program which will be elaborated in the next section, "Mantra." But in the main, the author insists that even sublime thoughts of God must be vanquished in contemplation, because thoughts of God are not God, and tend only to get between the seeker and God Himself.

The danger evangelicals would likely identify with a mentally vacuous, spiritually open state, is its susceptibility to the intrusion of demonic forces or other ungodly influences. It could be answered, however, that while *The Cloud* does advocate cognitive passivity for contemplatives, *The Cloud*'s intended audience are *Christians*. And in such a work, are Christian seekers really opening themselves up to any spiritual force, or to a very particular, all-powerful spiritual Force? The Englishman insists his students are not to fear violation by the evil one,

> for he will not dare come near you. Be he ever so cunning he is powerless to violate the inner sanctuary of your will, although he will sometimes attempt it by indirect means. Even an angel cannot touch your will directly. God alone may enter here.[291]

As the will of the seeker beats out with one aim, "God, God, God," can the devil be presumed able to infiltrate that will? The Englishman's presumption is that the devil is not able.

---

[291] Ibid.

But has he a basis for such a presumption? He makes no argument to support it. Effort, therefore, will be expended in his behalf.

As Christians engage in contemplative prayer in pursuit of God, and in so doing relieve their mind of content, opening themselves up to be filled with the Spirit of God, do they have any reasonable assurances that they will not be violated by evil spirits? Perhaps, according to the words of Jesus:

> Now suppose one of you fathers is asked by his son for a fish; he will not give him a snake instead of a fish, will he? Or if he is asked for an egg, he will not give him a scorpion, will he? If you then, being evil, know how to give good gifts to your children, how much more shall your heavenly Father give the Holy Spirit to those who ask Him?[292]

Jesus said that as His followers seek after the good gift of the company of and infilling of the Holy Spirit, they can *rest assured* that the Father will not disappoint them. When His children ask for good gifts He will not give evil.

Good biblical theology, however, requires that the entire word of God be consulted on any given issue. To reach a conclusion via one passage is unfounded if other relevant passages exist. So though Jesus offered assurances of security to believers in spiritual pursuits, by virtue of the Father's faithfulness and omnipotence, it must still be determined if empty-headed prayer is the means of choice or a legitimate means at all, in such pursuits.

The answer is this: The idea of mental vacuity, let alone the advocacy thereof, is not to be found in Holy Writ. Rather,

---

[292] Luke 11:11-13.

what is found is that spiritual exercises pertinent to *The Cloud* – namely, meditation and prayer – always have an attending noetic quality. Though some such states may include a suprarational element, such as tongues or ineffable visions, they are otherwise comprised of very rational *thoughts*. So whether suprarational or rational, believers' spiritual interactions with God, as represented in the Bible, are not characterized by thoughtlessness. Biblical prayer consist of speaking to or listening to God, neither of which are mentally vacuous states.[293] And biblical meditation is represented as: "meditating on Thy precepts, and regarding Thy ways,"[294] and "This book of the law shall not depart from your mouth, but you shall meditate on it day and night..."[295] So though not specifically spoken against, thoughtless mental states are neither advocated nor exemplified in Scripture.

In general, the Englishman's efforts to assure Christian seekers of safety from evil influences during prayer is good. To believe otherwise – that Satan or other evil spirits can somehow slip in the open door of a seeker's life while in the midst of prayer – seems to ascribe a power to Satan which is foreign to Scripture. The Bible does not teach a metaphysical dualism in which good and evil are equals pitted in an everlasting struggle. Rather, "You are from God, little children, and

> **Prayer is not a luck-of-the-draw gamble in which the responding force can never be anticipated.**

have overcome them (evil, antichrist spirits); because *greater*

---

[293] See Matthew 6:9-13; John 17; Acts 4:24-31.
[294] Psalm 119:15.
[295] Joshua 1:8.

is He who is in you than he who is in the world."[296] Prayer is not a luck-of-the-draw gamble in which the responding force can never be anticipated. Christians have assurances from the only omnipotent Force that they can rest in His protective power. To believe that evil forces will intrude themselves in such a scenario seems a violation of trust in God and in the power of His might.

It is crucial to keep in mind, however, that the above promises of protection are conditional. They apply only to God's spiritual children, born from above through faith in Christ. They apply only to those who act in accord with God's instructions. Non-Christians who delve into mysticism do not have such assurances or protection. They can easily fall prey to the wiles and whims, oppression or possession of the evil one and his minions.[297] But regenerate Christians are also susceptible to evil influence if they do not act in accord with God's instructions.

So what are "God's instructions" pertinent to this issue? And does *The Cloud*'s contemplative prayer violate any of these? As stated above, the Bible neither advocates nor exemplifies vacuous mental states. Rather, from its universal representation of prayer and meditation as noetic, it can justly be concluded that thoughtless prayer or meditation stand outside biblical parameters. Further, much of the Bible portrays God's people as in a state of spiritual warfare. Satan tempted Adam and Eve in the garden; Satan tested the faith of Job with many trials; and Peter tells Christians that their adversary, "the devil,

---

[296] 1 John 4:4. Parentheses and italics mine.
[297] Acts 19:13-16.

prowls about like a roaring lion, seeking someone to devour."[298] So clearly, God's people are not beyond the reach of evil. In light of this, Paul issues an injunction to Christians: they are to "put on the full armor of God," which includes "the sword of the Spirit, which is the word of God."[299] So not only does thoughtless prayer stand outside Scriptural parameters, but there are specific biblical instructions to realize and utilize the revealed truths of Scripture in combating evil.

With both of these factors in mind, it appears that the thoughtless nature of *The Cloud*'s contemplative prayer is not in accord with God's instruction, and therefore leaves its practitioners open to evil influences.

But as noted previously, the Englishman does agree that some contemplatives – novices – are susceptible to evil influences. Novice contemplatives may open themselves up to demonic deception by virtue of pride, straining effort, intellectual conceit, or a fanciful imagination.[300]

> **Evil influences/spirits…
> are to be thwarted not by
> *thoughtless* meditation,
> but by *thoughtful* medita-
> tion on the revealed
> truths of Scripture.**

While quoted earlier, the author's suggested antidote to such deception applies significantly to the issue now in question, and thus bears repeating:

> As these neophytes progress in the practices of the contemplative life, however, meditating faithfully on their own human frailty, the Passion of Christ, his transcendent good-

---

[298] 1 Peter 5:8.
[299] Ephesians 6:11, 17.
[300] Johnston, *The Cloud*, 105-106, 113-115.

ness, and the other truths of the interior life, Reason is gradually healed, regaining its rightful ascendancy over the Imagination.[301]

Evil influences/spirits, he says, are to be thwarted not by
thoughtless meditation, but by *thoughtful* meditation on the revealed truths of Scripture.   This markedly coincides with
Paul's instruction regarding spiritual warfare and the sword of
the Spirit being the word of God.

A question remains, however, as to how the Englishman
envisions applying this principle. If evil is thwarted by realizing, thinking upon, and acting upon the revealed truths of
Scripture, at what point must even these thoughts must be left
behind? He answers that, "a person who has long pondered
these things must eventually leave them behind beneath a
cloud of forgetting if he hopes to pierce *the cloud of unknowing* that lies between him and his God."[302]

In essence, then, *The Cloud* author sees biblical truths
as necessary in laying a foundation of proper thought and character in seekers. It is these which set seekers on the right
course. But having been grounded in the faith and having
come to realize a proper object, means, and result of their mystical pursuits, mystics may, or actually must he says, lay those
truths aside during contemplative prayer if they hope to reach
their goal.

But as this is his prescribed course, it must be countered
with the argument above: Thoughtlessness in prayer or meditation is nowhere advanced or exemplified in Scripture; and
the propositional truths of Scripture are to abide in the

---

[301] Ibid., 132.
[302] Ibid., 56.

thoughts of believers as an offensive weapon against the schemes of the devil. Consequently, it must be concluded that the *means* of contemplative prayer in *The Cloud* is erroneous to a degree corresponding to its advocacy of thoughtlessness.

Concerning the second aspect of 'thoughtlessness' in *The Cloud* – that which involves the *results* of contemplative prayer – attention will be given to its correlation or miscorrelation to biblical revelation. Namely, it was discovered in chapter four that Christian mystical experiences are typified by noetic content. Ezekiel and John the Revelator witnessed heavenly and futuristic scenes which they were in turn expected to convey in their writings. The result was profuse usage of metaphor, simile and other figurative language. In the third heaven, Paul heard words so exalted that humans were both incapable of and prohibited from speaking.

> **Though data perceived in the spiritual realm by biblical mystics was to varying degrees ineffable, it was nevertheless data; and though suprarational as it was experienced, it was not irrational.**

So though the data perceived in the spiritual realm by these biblical mystics was to varying degrees ineffable, it was nevertheless data; and though suprarational as it was experienced, it was not irrational.

Given then, that the result of the mystical task (unmediated encounter with God) is not meant to be devoid of content, how does *The Cloud* relate to this? On the face of it, many might at this juncture hold *The Cloud*'s mysticism as disparate with that of Scripture. After all, is not the focus of the Englishman "the cloud of *unknowing*"? In measure, such a response would be correct. During contemplation the author

does advocate training one's attention on the cloud of unknowing, of vacating the mind of thoughts. But it must recognized
that while attention is given to the cloud of unknowing as the
means of contemplation, the cloud is not the goal. He who lies
beyond the cloud is the goal. And in those rare moments God
may:

> touch you with a ray of his divine light which will pierce
> the cloud of unknowing between you and him. He will let
> you glimpse something of the ineffable secrets of his divine
> wisdom and your affection will seem on fire with his
> love.[303]

The successful contemplative perceives "something of the ineffable secrets" of God's "divine *wisdom*." And wisdom is
noetic; it involves cognitive content. The *result* of the Christian mysticism of the Englishman, then, corresponds with that
of Scripture.

MANTRA

Though he never uses the term, the Englishman's promo-
tion of monosyllabic words as mystical tools could easily be
equated with the 'mantra' of Hindu and Transcendental Meditation fame. He proposes that such a word, preferably simple
but significant, be used as a defense "in conflict and in
peace."[304] Elsewhere he suggests the word be used like a club
to ward off thoughts or other intrusions which raise themselves
up between the contemplative prayer and God. Similarly, the
Hindu mantra is "given by the master (guru) to a follower at

---

[303] Ibid., 84.
[304] Ibid., 56.

the time of initiation as a kind of weapon to ward off reasoning, thinking, and conceptualization."[305]

There exist, however, significant distinctions between the Englishman's club and the Eastern mantra. Whereas the mantra is designed to "unite the meditator with the divine within him,"[306] the club is intended to "beat upon the cloud of darkness above you and to subdue all distractions, consigning them to the cloud of forgetting beneath you,"[307] allowing the seeker to encounter the distinct, personal God. In addition, the mantra is "a sound *without meaning*, like OM, the vibrations of which lead to union with one's Source."[308] But the Christian contemplative is to "choose one (word) which is *meaningful* to you," and "should some thought go on annoying you demanding to know what you are doing, answer with this one word alone."[309]

So while Hindus and *The Cloud* use repeated vocal blasts as a means to their spiritual ends, both the *means* and the *object* in these respective exercises are distinct, as is presumably the *result*. The object of Hindus is union with the divine within, the Source. The object of *The Cloud* is encounter with the metaphysically distinct Creator, Yehovah. The means of Hindus is a meaningless, supposedly vibrationally significant vocal blast. The means of *The Cloud* is a meaningful vocal blast, a simple word which encompasses as much truth as possible, either that which is fully good – as in "God," or that which is fully evil – as in "sin."

---

[305] Lewis, *Transcendental Meditation*, 86. Parentheses mine.
[306] Ibid.
[307] Johnston, *The Cloud*, 56.
[308] Lewis, *Transcendental Meditation*, 86.
[309] Johnston, *The Cloud*, 56. Parentheses mine.

As for the result, there is no reason to believe that those from both traditions do not, upon occasion, break into the spiritual/mystical realm. But given the biblically disclosed reality of two domains within that realm – God's kingdom and that which Satan is allowed to rule; and given that God warns against taking up spiritual pursuits with a forbidden object, means, or result, it may be concluded that the 'domain' which non-Christian mystics experience is not God's.

> **Given the biblically disclosed reality of two domains within that realm... it may be concluded that the 'domain' which non-Christian mystics experience is not God's.**

Interestingly, it is through his monosyllabic club that the Englishman comes closest to redeeming his otherwise errant means of contemplation – thoughtlessness. How so? During the course of contemplation, he advises, "think only of God, the God who created you, redeemed you, and guided you to this work. Allow no other ideas about God to enter your mind. Yet even this is too much. A naked intent toward God, the desire for him alone is enough."[310]

So in this passage, he encourages his students to begin their prayer by thinking of God, but ends up advising them to give up even that thought – naked intent/desire is better. In other words, the will is to be set on course through thought, but then that thought is to be jettisoned. *But* he goes on to say, directly afterwards,

> If you want to gather all your *desire* into one simple word *that the mind can easily retain*, choose a short word rather

---

than a long one. A one-syllable word such as 'God' or
'love' is best. But choose *one that is meaningful* to you.
Then *fix it in your mind so that it will remain there come
what may...* [311]

Though these 'clubs' are presented as an option in contemplative prayer, what is significant is that the otherwise thoughtless
intent/will/desire which was alone to ascend toward God, is
here represented, in the form of the club, as *meaningful*, easily
retained by the *mind*, and it *is to stay with the prayer through
the course of contemplation*!

By making this concession, it seems the Englishman admits that contemplative prayer need not be as thoughtless as
he elsewise indicates. "Naked intent" can apparently have
some mental content to it. As a result, the means of mysticism
advocated in *The Cloud* cannot be dismissed as readily as it
otherwise could have.

CONCLUSIONS

The Cloud author admits that some who had taken up
something similar to a contemplative life fell into evil. These
persons became "slaves of the devil and the devil's contemplatives because they refused to listen to the counsel of authentic spiritual guides. They became hypocrites or heretics and
fell into frenzies and other wickedness."[312] Though the Englishman's students presumably appreciated the warning, they
could certainly have benefited from additional guidelines here.

---

[311] Ibid. Italics mine.
[312] Johnston, *The Cloud*, 73.

But the Englishman leaves it at that. He fails to mention how students might discern 'authentic spiritual guides' from counterfeits. With the profusion of purported 'spiritual guides' in existence today, the import of that unanswered question rings through the centuries. And it rings right through to the very thesis of this thesis.

Christian mysticism must begin and end with Bible-based rational activity. The object, means, and results of mysticism must square with the plain proclamations of Scripture. Authentic spiritual guides can be assessed by their correlation or miscorrelation with Scripture. Even the great apostle Paul was 'tested.' His Berean students "were more noble-minded than those in Thessalonica, for they received the word with great eagerness, *examining the Scriptures daily, to see whether these things were so.*"[313] Can we rightly do less?

But in the same breath, noble-*minded* Christians must never dispose of the mystical task because of its risky, suprarational nature. The rational propositions of the Bible declare the reality of suprarational knowledge and wisdom, a transcendent mystical realm, and advocate taking up the mystical task.

> **The rational propositions of the Bible declare the reality of suprarational knowledge and wisdom, a transcendent mystical realm, and advocate taking up the mystical task.**

God has given us minds and expects us to use them. God has given us spiritual capacities and expects us to use them.

---

[313] Acts 17:11. Italics mine.

May Christians on both ends of the spectrum move to embrace both the dynamism and mysticism of the Spirit, and the rule and rationality of the Word.

BIBLIOGRAPHY

Alexander, B. "Occult Philosophy and Mystical Experience." *SCP Journal* 6 (winter 1984): 13-19.

Almond, Philip C. *Mystical Experience and Religious Doctrine: An Investigation of the Study of Mysticism in World Religions*. New York: Mouton, 1982.

Alston, William P. *Swinburn on Faith and Belief.* Edited by A. Padgett. *Reason and the Christian Religion*. Oxford: Oxford University Press, 21-37, 1994.

Armstrong, Elizebeth. "Motives in the Writings of Julian of Norwich." *Mystics Quarterly* 16 (March 1990): 9-26.

Audi, Robert. *The Dimensions of Faith and the Demands of Reason*. Edited by E. Stump. *Reasoned Faith*. Ithaca, NY: Cornell University Press, 1993.

Barnes, L. Philip. "Introvertive Mystical Experiences." *Scottish Journal of Religion* 11 (Spring 1990): 5-17.

Barrett, Cyril. *The Logic of Mysticism*. Edited by M. Warner. *Religion and Philosophy*. Cambridge: Cambridge University Press, 1992.

Barrett, Earl. *A Christian Perspective of Knowing*. Kansas City MO: Beacon Hill Press, 1965.

Beckwith, C. A. "Mysticism," in *The New Schaff-Herzog Encyclopedia of Religious Knowledge*: Volume 8. Grand Rapid MI: Baker Book House, 1953.

Bergson, Henri. *The Two Sources of Morality and Religion*. Translated by R. Ashley Audra and Cloudesley Brereton, with the assistance of W. Horsfall Carter. New York: Holt and Company, 1935.

Braden, William. *The Private Sea: LSD and the Search for God*. Chicago: Quadrangle Books, 1967.

Brunner, Emil. *Dogmatics*. Volume I, *The Christian Doctrine of God*. Translated by Olive Wyon. Philadelphia: The Westminster Press, 1950.

_____. *Truth as Encounter*. Philadelphia: Westminster, 1964.

Buber, Martin. *I and Thou*. Translated by Ronald Gregor Smith. Edinburgh: T & T Clark, 1953.

Calgary Conference on Mysticism. *Mystics and Scholars*. Edited by Harold Coward and Terence Penelhum. Waterloo: Wilfred Laurier University Press, 1977.

Copleston, Frederick. *A History of Philosophy*. Vol. 2, *Medieval Philosophy*. New York: Doubleday, 1993.

Corduan, Winfried. *Mysticism: An Evangelical Option?* Grand Rapids: Zondervan, 1991.

_____. *Neighboring Faiths*. Downers Grove, IL: InterVarsity Press, 1998.

Cowan, Douglas E. *A Nakid Entent Unto God: A Source/Commentary on The Cloud of Unknowing*. Wakefield, NH: Longwood Academic, 1991.

D'arcy, Martin Cyril. *The Meeting of Love and Knowledge*. New York: Harper, 1957.

Dean, Stanley, R., ed. *Psychiatry and Mysticism*. Chicago: Nelson-Hall, 1975.

Drury, Nevill. *Dictionary of Mysticism and the Occult.* San Francisco: Harper & Row, 1985.

Dulles, Avery. *A History of Apologetics.* New York: Corpus Instrumentorum, 1971.

Dyrness, William. *Christian Apologetics in a World Community.* Downers Grove: Inter-Varsity Press, 1983.

Ellwood, Robert S. *Mysticism and Religion.* New York: Seven Bridges Press, 1999.

Erickson, Millard. *Christian Theology.* Grand Rapids: Baker Book House, 1985.

Ferguson, John. *An Illustrated Encyclopedia of Mysticism and the Mystery Religions.* New York: Seabury Press, 1977.

_____. *Encyclopedia of Mysticism and Mystery Religions.* New York: Crossroad, 1976.

Freemantle, Anne, ed. *The Protestant Mystics.* New York: Mentor, 1964.

Gaynor, Frank. *Dictionary of Mysticism.* New York: Philosophical Library, 1953.

Geivett, Douglas R., and Brendan Sweetman, eds. *Contemporary Perspectives on Religious Epistemology.* New York: Oxford University Press, 1992.

Groothuis, Douglas R. *Confronting the New Age.* Downers Grove IL: Intervarsity Press, 1988.

Hick, John. *The Rationality of Religious Belief.* Edited by R Geivett. *Contemporary Perspectives on Religious Epistemology.* New York: Oxford University Press, 1992.

Holm, Nils G., ed. *Religious Ecstasy*. Stockholm, Sweden: Distributed by Almqvist & Wiksell International, 1982.

Hughes, Thomas Hywel. *The Philosophic Basis of Mysticism*. Edinburgh: T. & T. Clark, 1937.

Idel, Moshe, and Bernard McGinn, eds. *Mystical Union and Monotheistic Faith*. New York: Collier Macmillan, 1989.

James, William. *Varieties of Religious Experience*. New York: Longmans, Green, and Co., 1928.

Jeffner, Anders. *The Difficult Limits of Logic*. Edited by A. Sharma. *God, Truth, and Reality*. New York: St. Martin's Press, 1993.

Johnson, Arthur, L. *Faith Misguided: Exploring the Dangers of Mysticism*. Chicago: Moody Press, 1988.

Johnston, William. *Christian Mysticism Today*. San Francisco: Harper & Row, 1984.

_____. *The Cloud of Unknowing and Book of Privy Counseling*. New York: Image Books, 1973.

Jones, Cheslyn, Geoffrey Wainwright, Edward Yarnold, eds. *The Study of Spirituality*. Oxford: Oxford University Press, 1986.

Jones, David Clyde. *Biblical Christian Ethics*. Grand Rapids: Baker Books, 1994.

Kanagaraj, Jey J. *Mysticism in the Gospel of John*. Sheffield Eng.: Sheffield Academic Press, 1998.

Katz, Steven T., ed. *Mysticism and Religious Traditions*. New York: Oxford University Press, 1983.

Kelly, Robert A. *Luther's Use of 1 Corinthians 14*. Edited by J. Bradley and R. Muller. *Church, Word and Spirit*. Grand Rapids: W. B. Eerdmans, 1987.

Knowles, David. *The English Mystical Tradition*. New York: Harper & Row, 1961.

Lawrence, Brother, and Frank Laubach. *Practicing His Presence*. Beaumont, TX: The SeedSowers, 1973.

Lewis, Gordon R. "Faith and History in St. Augustine." *Trinity Journal* 3 (Spring 1982) 39-50.

_____. *Testing Christianity's Truth Claims*. New York: University Press of America, 1990.

_____. *What Everyone Should Know About Transcendental Meditation*. Glendale CA: G/L Regal Books, 1975.

_____, and Bruce A. Demarest. *Integrative Theology*. Grand Rapids, MI: Zondervan Publishing House, 1996.

Llewelyn, Robert. *All Shall Be Well: The Spirituality of Julian of Norwich for Today*. New York: Paulist Press, 1982.

Louth, Andrew. *The Origins of the Christian Mystical Tradition*. Oxford: Clarendon Press, 1981.

McGinn, Bernard. "The Changing Shape of Late Medeival Mysticism." *Church History* 65 (June 1996): 197-219.

Meninger, William. *The Loving Search for God: Contemplative Prayer and The Cloud of Unknowing*. New York: Continuum, 1994.

Montgomery, John Warwick. "A Critique of William James' 'Varieties of Religious Experience.' " *The Shape of the Past*. Ann Arbor MI: Edwards, 1962.

Moreland, J. P. *Love God with All Your Mind*. Colorado Springs: NavPress, 1997.

Nagel, Thomas. *The Last Word*. New York: Oxford University Press, 1997.

Newport, John P. *The New Age Movement and the Biblical Worldview*. Grand Rapids: Eerdmans, 1998.

Nicoll, William Robertson. *The Garden of Nuts*. New York: A.C. Armstrong, 1905.

O'Brien, Elmer. *Varieties of Mystic Experience: An Anthology and Interpretation*. New York: Mentor-Omega, 1964.

Opperwall-Galluch, Nola J. "Reason; Reasoning; Reasonable," in *The International Standard Bible Encyclopedia*: Volume 4. Grand Rapids MI: Eerdmans, 1988.

Otto, Rudolf. *The Idea of the Holy; An Inquiry into the Non-rational Factor of the Idea of the Divine and Its Relation to the Rational*. Translated by John W. Harvey. New York: Oxford University Press, 1923.

_____. *Mysticism East and West*. Translated by Bertha L. Bracey and Richenda C. Payne. New York: Macmillan Company, 1932.

Pascal, Blaise. *Mind on Fire*. Edited by James M. Houston. Minneapolis: Bethany House, 1997.

Plantinga, Alvin. *Faith and Philosophy*. Grand Rapids: W. B. Eerdmans, 1964.

_____, and Nicholas Wolterstorff, eds. *Faith and Rationality*. Notre Dame: University of Notre Dame Press, 1983.

_____. *God and Other Minds*. Ithaca NY: Cornell University Press, 1967.

_____. *The Analytic Theist*. Grand Rapids: W. B. Eerdmans, 1998.

Pratt, James Bisset. *The Religious Consciousness: The Psychological Study*. New York: Macmillan, 1928.

Ramm, Bernard. *The Witness of the Spirit*. Grand Rapids: Eerdmans, 1959.

Rhodes, Ron. "Close Encounters of the Celestial Kind." *Christian Research Journal* 17 (Spring 1995): 17-23.

Ringgren, Helmer. "Mysticism," in *The Anchor Bible Dictionary*: Volume 4. New York: Doubleday, 1992.

Runzo, Joseph, and Craig K. Ihara, eds. *Religious Experience and Religious Belief*. Lanham MD: University Press of America, 1986.

Schleiermacher, Friedrich. *Pioneer of Modern Theology*. Minneapolis: Fortress Press, 1991.

_____. *The Christian Faith*. Edited by H. R. Mackintosh and J. S. Stewart. Edinburgh: T & T Clark, 1948.

Schmiel, D. G. "Martin Luther's Relationship to the Mystical Tradition." *Concordia Journal* 9 (March 1983): 45-49.

Sire, James W. *The Universe Next Door*. Downers Grove, IL: Intervarsity Press, 1997.

Sproul, R. C., John Gerstner and Arthur Lindsley. *Classical Apologetics*. Grand Rapids: Zondervan Publishing House, 1984.

Staal, Frits. *Exploring Mysticism: A Methodological Essay*. Berkeley: University of California Press, 1975.

Stace, W. T. *Mysticism and Philosophy*. Philadelphia: Lippencott, 1960.

_____. *Religion and the Modern Mind*. Philadelphia: Lippencott, 1952.

_____. *Time and Eternity*. Princeton: Princeton University Press, 1952.

Starke, Linda, ed. *State of the World 1999.* New York: W. W. Norton & Company, 1999.

Sylvia, Sister Mary. *Pauline and Johannine Mysticism.* London: Darton, Longman & Todd, 1964.

Tozer, A. W. "The Divine Indwelling." *Alliance Life* 130 (November 1995): 10.

Underhill, Evelyn. *Mysticism.* New York: Noonday Press, 1955.

_____. *The Life of the Spirit and the Life of Today.* San Francisco: Harper & Row, 1986.

_____. *The Mystics of the Church.* New York: Schocken Books, 1964.

Wainwright, William J. "Religious Experience and Language," in *Companion Encyclopedia of Theology.* Edited by P. Byrne, and others. London: Routledge, 1995.

Walsh, James S. J., ed. *The Cloud of Unknowing.* New York: Paulist Press, 1981.

Ward, Benedicta. "Mysticism and Devotion in the Middle Ages," in *Companion Encyclopedia of Theology.* Edited by P. Byrne, and others. London: Routledge, 1995.

Warfield, B.B. "Mysticism and Christianity." *Biblical and Theological Studies.* Nutley NJ: Presbyterian and Reformed, 1952.

Windeatt, Barry A. *English Mystics of the Middle Ages.* Cambridge: Cambridge University Press, 1994.

Wolterstorff, Nicholas P. *Is Reason Enough?* Edited by R. Geivett. *Contemporary Perspectives on Religious Epistemology.* New York: Oxford University Press, 1992.

Woods, Richard. *Understanding Mysticism*. Garden City NY: Image Books, 1980.

Woolf, Henry Bosley, ed. *Webster's New Collegiate Dictionary*. Springfield MA: C. & G. Merriam Company, 1964.

Woolsley, Linda Mills. "Saints, Mystics, and the Ordinary Christian Life." *Perspectives* 11 (December 1996): 16-18.

Young, Warren C. *A Christian Approach to Philosophy*. Wheaton IL: Van Kampen, 1954.

Zaehner, R. C. *Mysticism Sacred and Profane*. London: Oxford University Press, 1971.

_____. *Zen, Drugs, and Mysticism*. New York: Pantheon Books, 1972.

AUTHOR

The son of an oilfield laboring father and retail clerk mother, DCTopp was the first in his family – immediate or extended – to graduate from college.

He was later adopted by the Father, having been wooed by the Spirit and won by the Son. Though intimate with the trials and travails of being human, since infused with new and abundant life from the Creator, DCTopp has sought to honor Him, grow closer to Him and His ways, and introduce others to the Wonder Maker who made us all.

He holds that whether you know or admit it, all of life is infused with and fundamentally influenced by things spiritual. Hence, DCTopp pursues his ends by speaking to things of the spirit, spirit & science, and spirit & society.

TOPIC INDEX

waiting, as a means to the
  mystical task, 84, 92
Walsh, James S. J. , 50, 120-
  122, 124
will, the, 48-50, 125, 134
Windeatt, Barry A., 20
word of God, 13, 15n5, 45, 117,
  126, 129-130
works, good, 26, 32-34, 60,
  108-111
worldview, 15, 60, 63-64
worship
  distinctions of, 64, 92

means to the mystical task,
  as, 65, 84-85, 92
result of the mystical task,
  as, 95
Wyclif, John, 23

Yehovah, as ordinate mystical
  object, 54, 54n109, 65, 80,
  83, 85, 92-93, 114, 133
yoga, 63, 65

Zwingli, Huldrych, 68

SCRIPTURE INDEX

13:10-11 (79n164)
22:36-40 (108n237,
  110n247)
27:51 (80n168)

1 Peter
    4:10 (69n143)
    5:8 (129n298)

2 Peter
    1:4 (123n288)

Psalms
    4:4 (93n219)
    50:21-22 (94n223)
    82:6 (123n288)
    119 (93n219)
    119:15 (127n294)
    143:5 (93n219)

Revelation
    1:10 (91n213)
    2:4 (108n238)
    18:23 (101n234)
    19:10 (92n214, 95n225)
    22:9 (95n225)

Romans
    1:11 (69n143)
    1:22-25 (92n214)
    5:15 (69n143)
    6:11 (97n227)
    7:14-25 (122n284)
    8:26-27 (100n230)
    16:25 (67n137)

1 Samuel
    28 (93n220)

1 Timothy
    4:1 (94n224)

www.ingramcontent.com/pod-product-compliance
Lightning Source LLC
LaVergne TN
LVHW011235080426
835509LV00005B/509